STAR MAPS

FOR SOUTHERN AFRICA

AN EASY GUIDE TO
THE NIGHT SKIES

ALBERT JANSEN

Struik Publishers
(a division of New Holland Publishing (South Africa) (Pty) Ltd)
Cornelis Struik House
80 McKenzie Street
Cape Town 8001

New Holland Publishing is a member of Johnnic
Communications Ltd.
Visit us at **www.struik.co.za**
Log on to our photographic website
www.imagesofafrica.co.za for an African experience.

First published in 2004

10 9 8 7 6 5 4 3 2 1

Publishing manager: Pippa Parker
Managing editor: Helen de Villiers
Editor: Lorraine Cox
Design director: Janice Evans
Designer: Robin Cox
Cover design: Robin Cox

Reproduction by Hirt & Carter Cape (Pty) Ltd
Printed and bound by Sing Cheong Printing Company Ltd

ISBN 1 77007 005 2

**Front cover and title page: Comet Hyakutake
with bright star Arcturus
Back cover: The Carina Nebula with two star clusters
This page: The Small Magellanic Cloud**

CONTENTS

The magnificent Carina Nebula with two clusters

INTRODUCTION

Stargazing can be great fun, especially if you are using well-designed star maps. Unfortunately, most star maps are drawn to such a small scale that huge constellations appear tiny on the map. Often, just one map is used to show the *whole* sky at a certain moment. This guide is different in that it has been designed to make stargazing simple. All its maps are drawn to a generous and intuitive scale.

HOW TO USE THIS BOOK

Star Maps for Southern Africa features 96 full-page star maps. Selecting the map you need depends on the *time* and the *month* of your observation and on the *direction* in which you are looking.

There are twelve sets of eight maps. Each set applies to a number of different months, depending on the time of night that the sky is being viewed. Set 1, for example, is equally valid for use at 05h in September, 03h in October, 01h in November, 23h in December and 21h in January.

Our view of the sky is ever-changing, so for every two hours each night (and for each successive month), a different set of eight maps applies. For example, at 21h in January , Set 1 applies; in January at 23h, Set 2 applies, at 01h, Set 3 applies; at 03h, Set 4 applies, and so on. Similarly, for February at 21h, Set 2 applies, at 23h, Set 3 applies, etc.

Each one of the eight maps in Sets 1 to 12 shows a part of the sky in detail, and represents one of the eight principal directions (N, NE, E, SE, S, SW, W, NW). As you examine the entire sky and turn slowly through 360°, you will be able to use each of the eight maps in succession.

Selecting your set of star maps

	19h	21h	23h	01h	03h	05h
Jan		1	2	3	4	
Feb		2	3	4	5	
Mar		3	4	5	6	7
Apr	3	4	5	6	7	8
May	4	5	6	7	8	9
Jun	5	6	7	8	9	10
Jul	6	7	8	9	10	11
Aug		8	9	10	11	12
Sep		9	10	11	12	1
Oct		10	11	12	1	2
Nov		11	12	1	2	
Dec		12	1	2	3	

In order to find the appropriate set of star maps for a given two-hour period at any time of night in the year, you will need to consult the table above. This table also appears on the inside front cover for ease of reference. You will notice that the column for 21h or 9 pm stands out. This is because 9 pm is the most popular time of night for stargazing.

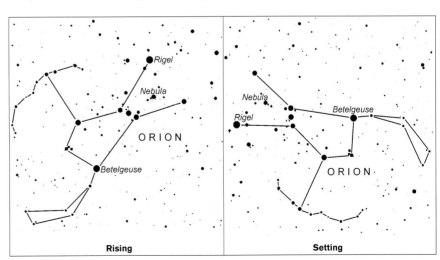

Each set of maps features a prominent constellation (or more than one), shown rising and setting. Orion, above, is illustrated in Star Maps Set 1.

SKY ORIENTATION

- East is where the Sun rises; west is where the Sun sets.
- If you face west, north is to your right and south is to your left.
- If you face east, north is to your left and south is to your right.
- All maps are drawn to a standard scale for ease of use.
- For each month of the year, the set of eight maps gives the view in each principal direction: N, NE, E, SE, S, SW, W, and NW.
- The stars on the horizon appear near the bottom of each map, and stars in the sky directly above you appear near the top.

Introducing the maps

The introduction to each set of star maps begins with an illustration of one constellation (or more) that is prominent in the sky at that time. Two views are given (one rising and one setting). The apparent difference between rising and setting is a direct result of the Earth's daily rotation, which makes the constellation appear to 'topple over'. Try to remember the shape of each constellation while ignoring the apparent tilts.

A short description and summary of the sky follows, alerting the user to stars and constellations, as well as addressing frequently asked questions.

New Moon tables

Each introduction includes a table that lists the dates of future new Moons (nights when there will be no hindrance from moonlight, and therefore the stars will be more visible). Using these tables, you can select a moonless night as far ahead as 2022 to see the stars and make the best use of your star maps. Choose nights that are near to one of the dates listed.

After 2022, it is still possible to use the new Moon tables. Simply deduct 19 (or any multiple of 19) from the year you are in and use the tables again. For example to find the new Moon for January 2052, deduct 38 (19 x 2) from the year 2052 to bring you back to 2014. This calculation is accurate to within one day.

Using the star maps

All star maps have been drawn using a standard scale, and are *working* documents. They depict the stars as black points on a white ground, enabling you to make notes on the maps. You may connect the stars in a way that appeals to you, or pencil in a planet's motion over time.

The maps show all stars that are visible to the naked eye when the sky is perfectly dark. The brightest stars are rendered bigger and bolder than faint stars (to make obvious groups in the sky stand out) and are labelled with proper names. Objects that particularly merit binocular investigation are depicted on the maps as grey, fuzzy spots (indicating certain clusters, nebulae and the galaxy in Andromeda) or are outlined in small crosses (indicating the two Magellanic Clouds).

Turn to the appropriate set of star maps for your current month and time of night. Then choose the right map for the direction in which you are looking (N, NE, and so on). Try to identify some of the brightest stars. Then try to find the patterns or groups of stars called constellations, starting with the brightest. As a rule, the brightest may guide you to less conspicuous constellations. Look for particular shapes and star alignments, such as the three stars in a row that comprise Orion's Belt.

SEPTEMBER		OCTOBER		NOVEMBER		DECEMBER		**JANUARY**	
06h	05h	04h	03h	02h	01h	00h	23h	22h	**21h**	20h

At the foot of each star map is a guide, such as the one above, that shows the months and times at which the map applies. This information can also be found in the table 'How to select your star maps' on the inside front cover/page 5.

STARGAZING IN PRACTICE

To enjoy the starry sky at its very best, the sky should be perfectly dark and your eyes should have been given the chance to adapt completely to this unspoilt darkness. Finding and waiting for a suitable level of darkness and going through the process of 'dark adaptation' require time and patience.

Dark skies

Twilight and moonlight are two natural sources of sky brightness that can easily be avoided by stargazing at the right time. Stargazing is most effective during the darkest hours of the month – more than two hours after sunset and more than two hours before sunrise, and in the week around new Moon.

In many cases, man-made light pollution is far more intrusive than twilight and moonlight. Light from small towns may interfere with night viewing some fifty kilometres beyond their boundaries, while big cities pollute the night sky two or three hundred kilometres beyond their limits. One *can* view the brightest stars from cities and towns but keen star-watchers will be able to avoid light pollution only by moving to a remote, rural setting such as in the Karoo.

Dark adaptation

Normal eyes can adapt to widely different levels of brightness. We can easily see anything from a white cloud in sunlight to thousands of dim stars in a night sky. In fact, a sunlit cloud is one hundred million times brighter than an unpolluted, dark sky.

Remember that even a small glare makes your adjustment to the dark difficult. Nightlights such as street-lamps – even a few kilometres away – must be kept out of view. Headlamps of passing cars will spoil your 'dark adaptation' for quite a time, so keep away from roads.

Full adaptation to darkness takes between 30 and 45 minutes (the length of twilight). Stargazers should wait long enough to increase night vision to its optimum.

Inexperienced stargazers may prefer to find bright stars in a twilit or moonlit night sky. When the sky is not completely dark it will appear less crowded with stars, so less confusing to a beginner.

Equipment for stargazing

Use as little light as necessary to read the star maps, in order to preserve your adaptation to the dark. Use the smallest torch you can get, such as a penlight torch, and cover the lens with red cellophane or plastic to produce a dim red light that does not interfere with night vision. A piece of dark red cotton over the lens works just as well. Keep a standard-sized torch at hand for emergencies (such as losing something in the grass), but restrict its use to real emergencies.

All types of binoculars will help you to see the stars, but those with larger lenses bring more light into your eyes and therefore make dimmer objects visible. A high magnification can be useful, but requires stability during viewing. Image-stabilized binoculars are a recent and most welcome development, but are still very expensive. An important consideration is simply the instrument's weight. For the purpose of astronomy, the 7 x 50 is a good compromise. It magnifies 7 times and has two lenses of 50 mm diameter. Ultimately, it is best to use the type of binoculars that feels comfortable to you.

Focus your binoculars carefully, using the central wheel for your left eye, and the eyepiece adjuster for your right eye. Focus until the stars look like pinpoints. To keep your binoculars stable, you may wish to use a tripod with a clamp. Alternatively you could turn a dining-chair back to front, and sit down, supporting your elbows on its back while you view the stars.

The shape and movement of the Earth

Both the curvature and spinning of the Earth must be taken into account when reading the star maps and comparing them to the night sky.

Strictly speaking, the star maps apply to central South Africa, more specifically to Kimberley. North of Kimberley, the northern stars rise higher than is shown, while those in the South sink deeper. South of Kimberley some northern stars will never rise, and some in the South will never set.

These effects are caused by curvature of the Earth. As the Earth turns on its axis once a day, the view of the sky changes hourly, and because the Earth orbits the Sun once a year, there is a month-to-month change as well. The table on page 5 is based on the combined effect of these movements. Therefore, your selection of maps depends on the month and hour of observation.

THE STARRY SKY

There is a phenomenal number of fixed and moving objects in the sky. Some objects, such as meteors and artificial satellites, move across the sky in split seconds or minutes. Other objects such as our Moon and planets undergo marked changes of position and/or appearance over days or weeks.

A long exposed photograph of the Southern Cross constellation with several clusters

The Moon and planets

The Moon is not shown on the star maps because its position differs from day to day as it moves around the Earth. The planets are also not shown on the star maps because, like Earth, they constantly orbit the Sun. Their positions change from month to month and from year to year.

The Moon and planets do not shine by their own light. We see them only because they are illuminated by the Sun. 'Moonlight' or the light reflected by the Moon takes just over one second to reach the Earth, but light reflected from the planets can take minutes or even hours to reach us. These minutes and hours represent distances of up to many million kilometres. Yet, compared to the stars, the planets are close at hand. If stars were described as being in far-away cities, planets would be in the back yard. Working to this scale, the Moon would be only 10 millimetres away.

The Sun and other stars

The Sun is a star and, like all stars, is a huge, glowing ball of gases. Our Sun looks so big and bright because, compared to other stars, it is extremely near to Earth: its rays reach us in just over eight minutes, while light rays from other stars travel many years before they can be seen.

Stars form when large clouds of gas and dust contract owing to gravitational forces, triggering a nuclear reaction that gives off heat and light. Stars die when their nuclear fuel is depleted, causing their collapse.

The end of a star

Lightweight stars end their lives by blowing off their outer layers as a dim, greenish nebula or gas cloud, and contracting their inner parts to a so-called white dwarf – an extremely hot, dense object, about the size of Earth, but with the mass of the Sun.

Heavy, fast-burning stars end their lives in a gigantic 'supernova' explosion caused by the sudden collapse of their core. Such stars implode and rebound, and shoot large amounts of material into space. The collapsing centre contracts into an exceedingly dense neutron star that may, in more extreme cases, turn into a black hole, in which the pull of gravity becomes strong enough to prevent even light from escaping.

Checklist of the brightest stars

	Stars	Constellations	
	(Sun)		✓
1	Sirius	Brightest of Canis Maior	
2	Canopus	Brightest of Carina	
3	Alpha Centauri	Brightest 'Pointer'	
4	Arcturus	Brightest of Bootes	
5	Vega	Brightest of Lyra	
6	Capella	Brightest of Auriga	
7	Rigel	Brightest of Orion (blue)	
8	Procyon	Brightest of Canis Minor	
9	Achernar	Brightest of Eridanus	
10	Betelgeuse	Second of Orion (red)	
11	Beta Centauri	Second 'Pointer'	
12	Altair	Brightest of Aquila	
13	Alpha Crucis	Brightest of Crux	
14	Aldebaran	Brightest of Taurus	
15	Spica	Brightest of Virgo	
16	Antares	Brightest of Scorpius (red)	
17	Pollux	Brightest 'twin' of Gemini	
18	Fomalhaut	Brightest of Piscis Austrinus	
19	Beta Crucis	Second of Crux	
20	Deneb	Brightest of Cygnus	
21	Regulus	Brightest of Leo	
22	Epsilon Canis Maioris	Second of Canis Maior	
23	Castor	Second 'twin' of Gemini	
24	Gamma Crucis	Third of Crux	
25	Lambda Scorpii	Second of Scorpius ('sting')	
26	Gamma Orionis	Third of Orion (near 'shield')	
27	Beta Tauri	Second of Taurus (a 'horn')	
28	Beta Carinae	Second of Carina (near Volans)	
29	Epsilon Orionis	Centre of Orion's Belt	
30	Alpha Gruis	Brightest of Grus	
31	Zeta Orionis	Sirius's side of Orion's Belt	
32	Gamma-2 Velorum	Brightest of Vela	
33	Epsilon Ursae Maioris	Brightest of Ursa Maior	

'Shooting stars'

If you see a star-like object moving across the sky, you can be certain it is not a 'shooting star'. It will be a meteor, an aircraft or an artificial satellite.

Meteors are often referred to as 'shooting stars'. They move quickly and last for just a few seconds. The 'shooting-star' effect is caused by sand grains or pebbles, which enter our atmosphere at very high speeds (tens of kilometres per second). Friction converts their energy into light and heat. In fact, before these particles burn up, they behave like microscopic planets that move in orbit around the Sun.

An **aircraft** in motion can be identified in the night sky by its red and green lights, although you cannot often hear its engines.

A slow-moving 'star', visible for several minutes, is one of the approximately ten thousand **artificial satellites** that litter our night sky. They have been sent into space by governments for a multitude of purposes, such as for political propaganda, military reconnaissance, telecommunication, navigation (GPS), Earth Science research, astronomical research, and to track weather patterns and monitor agriculture. However, most of the satellites become almost indestructable 'space junk' because they orbit the Earth at heights where there is almost no atmospheric friction. This causes them to survive for thousands of years. We see them only when they are lit by the Sun as they pass by. They appear to fade away as soon as they enter the Earth's shadow.

The brightest stars

The apparent brightness of a star depends on its temperature, its size and its distance from the Earth. The brightest stars are not always nearby; they may look close because they are very big and hot, but may be quite distant. Conversely, a small, cool star may look bright because it is close to the Earth.

The table on page 9 lists the brightest stars in the sky, beginning with our Sun. It is the brightest star because it is easily the nearest although, in the context of the Milky Way Galaxy, our Sun is of only average size and temperature. Its mass, age and composition make our Sun an average star in all respects.

Real groups of stars

Stars are usually formed in groups that are tied together by gravity and vary in age, such as multiple stars and clusters. Young clusters contain all kinds of stars that burn at different rates, including extremely bright, short-living stars, sometimes referred to as 'big-spenders'. As clusters grow older, they gradually lose their brightest stars. The oldest clusters are billions of years old and have no very bright stars left.

Galaxies

By far the largest star groupings we know of are galaxies, holding between one billion and one trillion stars each. The Universe is as filled with galaxies as our Milky Way Galaxy is crowded with stars. Only three neighbouring galaxies are near enough to be seen with the naked eye: the Andromeda Galaxy and the two Magellanic Clouds.

The Sun is part of the Milky Way Galaxy, as are all individual stars and star clusters that you can see with the naked eye or through binoculars.

The Small Magellanic Cloud

The Large Magellanic Cloud

Multiple stars

The majority of stars have one to five partners. Our home star, the Sun, is a single star, and therefore is rather an exception to the rule.

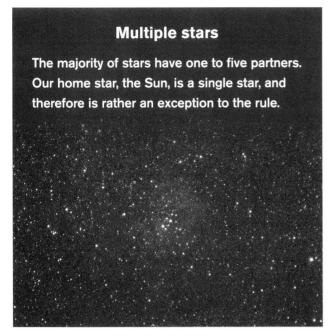

The Rosette Nebula

Open star clusters

Groupings of a few hundred single stars – in general without 'steady partners' – are called 'open clusters'. Many of them are indicated on the star maps, for example, the Pleiades and the Hyades, as well as Coma Berenices. They look impressive through binoculars. The structure of open clusters is mainly loose and irregular.

Most open clusters we know of are relatively young. Some were formed only two or three million years ago. They contain extremely bright stars (the 'big spenders') that will burn out long before the cluster has been able to fully develop.

Globular star clusters

Globular clusters are quite different from open clusters. They contain up to a few million stars, show a perfect spherical symmetry, and have centres that can be very crowded. It is estimated that some globular clusters have existed for about 13 billion years, which is nearly three times longer than the Sun and the Earth.

Two globular clusters are marked on the maps: one in Centaurus, and the other near the Small Magellanic Cloud. They appear as fuzzy stars to the naked eye, and show up as fuzzy balls through binoculars. To see their brightest stars, you need a telescope.

Our Milky Way Galaxy

The name Milky Way refers to the path of star 'clouds' that forms a distinct arch in the sky. It is obvious to the naked eye when the sky is dark enough (without twilight, moonlight or light pollution). The Milky Way Galaxy consists of well over a hundred billion stars, ranging from bright to very faint. All these stars (including our Sun) are arranged in a flat, rotating disk that contains several spiral 'arms'. All individual stars and nearby clusters that we see with the naked eyes are part of our home galaxy. Light takes one thousand centuries to cross it. The Sun and its planets are near the edge of the Milky Way, which is but one of billions of galaxies above and around us.

The Zodiac and constellations

The Zodiac is an imaginary highway along which we see the Moon and planets move. Its full circle stretches through the constellations Aries, Taurus, Gemini, Cancer, Leo, Virgo, Libra, Scorpius, Ophiuchus, Sagittarius, Capricornus, Aquarius and Pisces, where it links up again with Aries. At any moment only one half of this circle is visible above our horizon.

Constellation names are traditional names that have been given to groups or patterns of stars. They have helped stargazers down the centuries to identify and remember star patterns. Constellations are useful tools that 'divide' the sky into 'manageable chunks', similar to the way that the Earth is apportioned into countries. Using this analogy, bright stars are 'big cities' and the dim ones, 'small towns'. Countries can be ancient or new, and the same holds for constellations. Some are mentioned in the Biblical Book of Job and by Homer. More than half are over two thousand years old. Some forty new ones have been identified in the southern skies.

Planets

A bright 'star' in a constellation, not marked on the map, is a planet. Pencil in its position between the stars each night and track it over a week or two. Usually its motion will become obvious – a sure sign that it is a planet.

SET 1
JANUARY AT 21H

USE ALSO IN DECEMBER AT 23H, NOVEMBER AT 01H, OCTOBER AT 03H, SEPTEMBER AT 05H

AT OTHER TIMES OF THE NIGHT IN JANUARY, USE: SET 2 AT 23H, SET 3 AT 01H, AND SET 4 AT 03H

HIGHLIGHT OF THE SKY TONIGHT

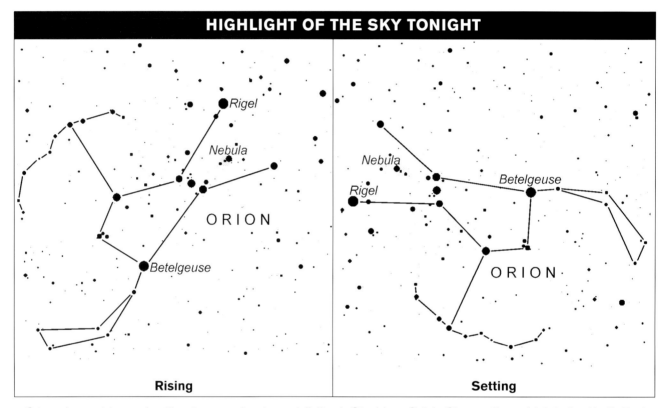

Rising

Setting

Orion, shown rising and setting, is a prominent constellation in Star Maps Set 1. *Observe it very high in the North-East.*

A guided tour of the sky

The bright star Capella, part of the Auriga constellation, twinkles rather low in the **North**. The Perseus constellation lies to the left of it. Aldebaran is the red star in the constellation of Taurus, visible much higher than Perseus. The Hyades cluster (shaped like an 'A') lies immediately to the left of Aldebaran. Further left and a little lower is another cluster, the Pleiades or the Seven Sisters. Use binoculars to view these clusters in detail.

High up in the **North-East**, the Orion constellation is most prominent. Its brightest stars are of different colours: Rigel is bluish, while Betelgeuse is red. Not far

from Orion's Belt (the three stars in a row) you can find the famous Orion Nebula, a gas cloud from which new stars are forming. Use binoculars for a better view. Below Orion is Gemini; its Twins, Castor and Pollux, are rather close to the horizon. Somewhat right of Gemini is the bright star Procyon.

High in the **East** is Sirius (or the Dog Star), part of the constellation Canis Maior. Sirius is the brightest star, not counting the Sun, and is pure white.

Nearly as bright as Sirius is Canopus, high up in the **South-East**. Below it, the Milky Way is quite obvious. Below Canopus you can find the False Cross (*not* a constellation) and further down is the beautiful Nebula in Carina. Close to the horizon is Crux, the 'real' Southern Cross constellation.

Both Magellanic Clouds are visible to the **South**. They are dwarf galaxies relatively close to the one we live in. Their faint light has travelled roughly two thousand centuries to reach us. Binoculars reveal some detail, but a telescope shows some of their individual stars.

Quite high in the **South-West**, the star Achernar lies at one end of the huge constellation Eridanus. The other end of Eridanus is near Rigel in Orion. Much lower you can see the constellation of Grus, with the Pavo constellation to its left and the star Fomalhaut to its right.

The sky in the **West** looks rather empty, where our view is almost perpendicular to the Milky Way. This observation proves that our galaxy is far from spherical – on the contrary, it is a very flat disk. You can find only one rather bright star in the West, called Diphda (in the constellation of Cetus).

In the **North-West** the constellation of Aries is hard to identify, and Pisces (to its left) is even more difficult. The same can be said of Cetus, although it fills a large part of the sky. Near the horizon, you can see some stars of the constellations Pegasus and Andromeda.

Hot and cool stars

Stars have widely differing temperatures. The coolest stars look red, such as Betelgeuse in Orion (2 500° C). The hottest look bluish-white, such as Rigel in Orion (15 000° C). Our Sun is a golden or yellow star of average temperature (6 000° C).

Part of the Orion constellation

Bright and dim stars

Some bright-looking stars are close by. Other stars that look equally bright are so far away that their light takes over one thousand years to reach us. These distant, bright stars produce such enormous amounts of light that they burn their nuclear fuel in a relatively short time (a few million years). The best example is Rigel, which looks almost as bright as Alpha Centauri, although it is hundreds of times farther away. In contrast, many neighbouring stars are too dim to be seen. Such faint, slow-burning stars spare their energy and grow extremely old before they die.

NEW MOON IN JANUARY

The week around new Moon is ideal for stargazing. A January new Moon will occur:

Year	Day	Year	Day
2004	21st	2014	1st & 30th
2005	10th	2015	20th
2006	29th	2016	10th
2007	19th	2017	28th
2008	8th	2018	17th
2009	26th	2019	6th
2010	15th	2020	24th
2011	4th	2021	13th
2012	23rd	2022	2nd
2013	11th		

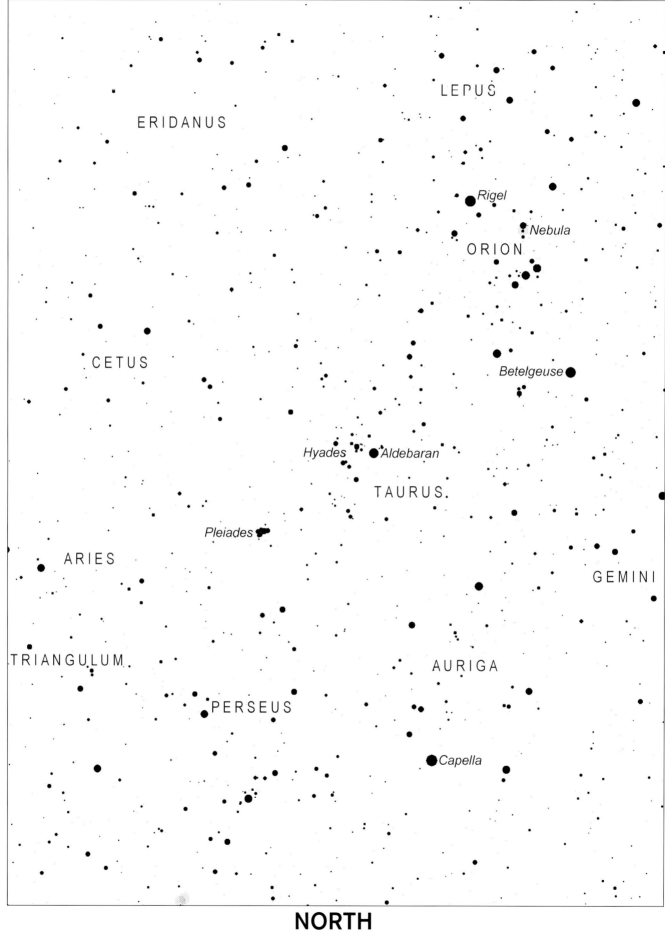

LEPUS

ERIDANUS

Rigel

Nebula

ORION

Betelgeuse

CETUS

Hyades ● Aldebaran

TAURUS.

Pleiades

ARIES

GEMINI

TRIANGULUM

AURIGA

PERSEUS

Capella

NORTH

SEPTEMBER	OCTOBER	NOVEMBER	DECEMBER	**JANUARY**	
06h 05h 04h	03h 02h	01h 00h	23h 22h	**21h**	20h

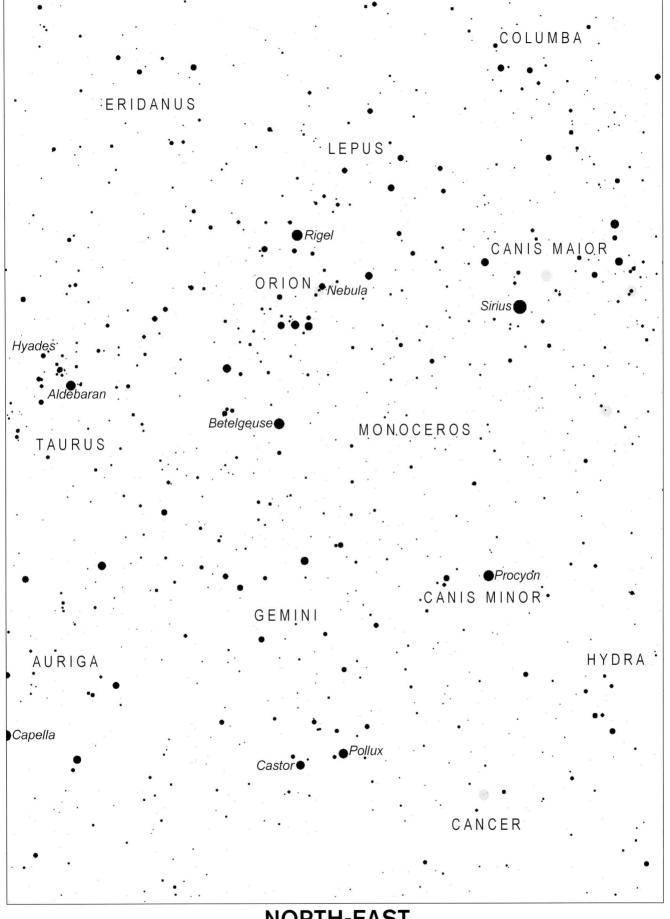

COLUMBA

ERIDANUS

LEPUS

Rigel

CANIS MAIOR

ORION *Nebula*

Sirius

Hyades

Aldebaran

Betelgeuse

MONOCEROS

TAURUS

CANIS MINOR

Procyon

GEMINI

AURIGA

HYDRA

Capella

Pollux

Castor

CANCER

NORTH-EAST

SEPTEMBER		OCTOBER		NOVEMBER		DECEMBER		JANUARY	
06h	05h	04h	03h	02h	01h	00h	23h	22h	**21h**	20h

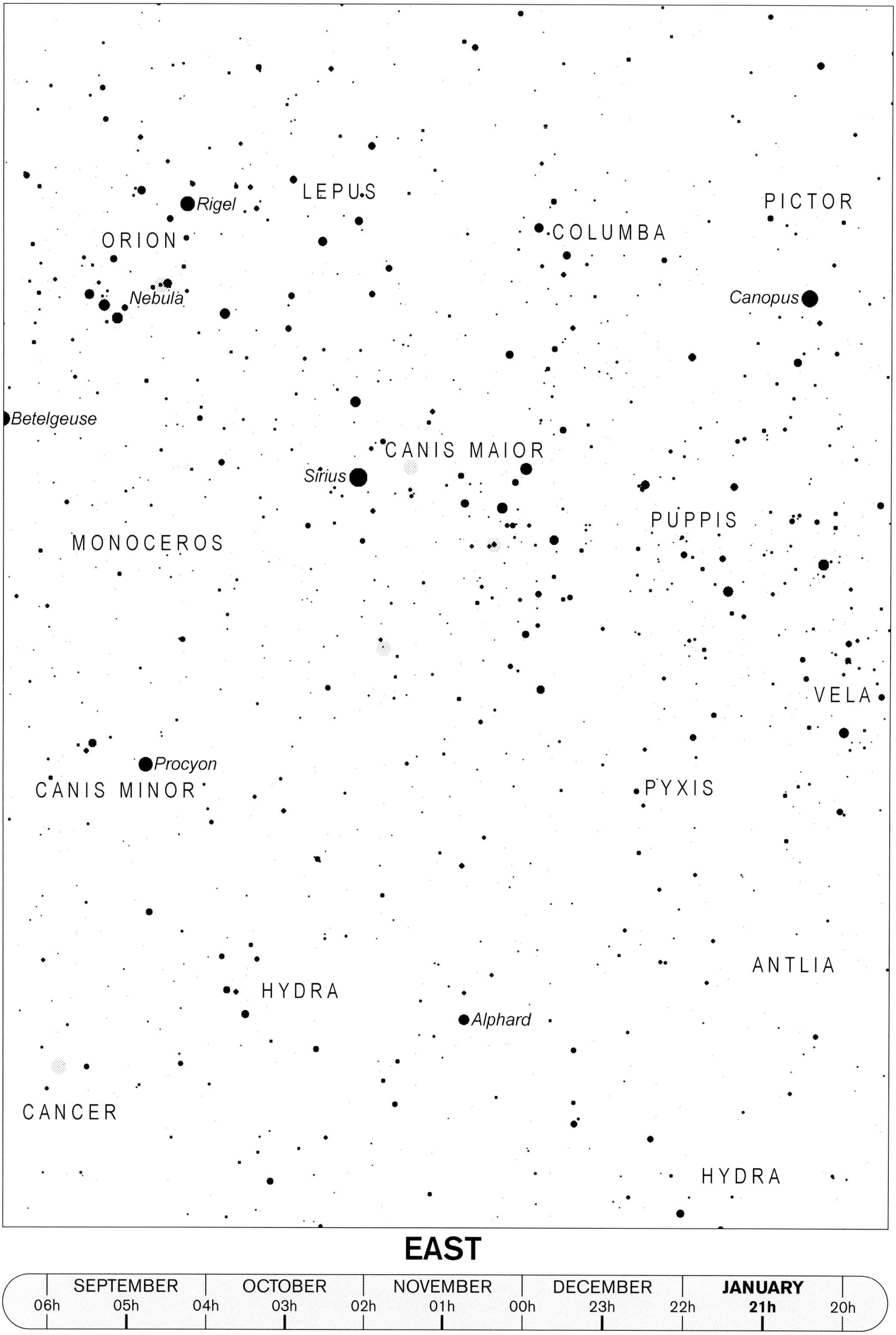

LEPUS

PICTOR

COLUMBA

ORION

●Rigel

●*Nebula*

Canopus ●

●Betelgeuse

CANIS MAIOR

Sirius ●

PUPPIS

MONOCEROS

VELA

●*Procyon*

CANIS MINOR

PYXIS

ANTLIA

HYDRA

●*Alphard*

CANCER

HYDRA

EAST

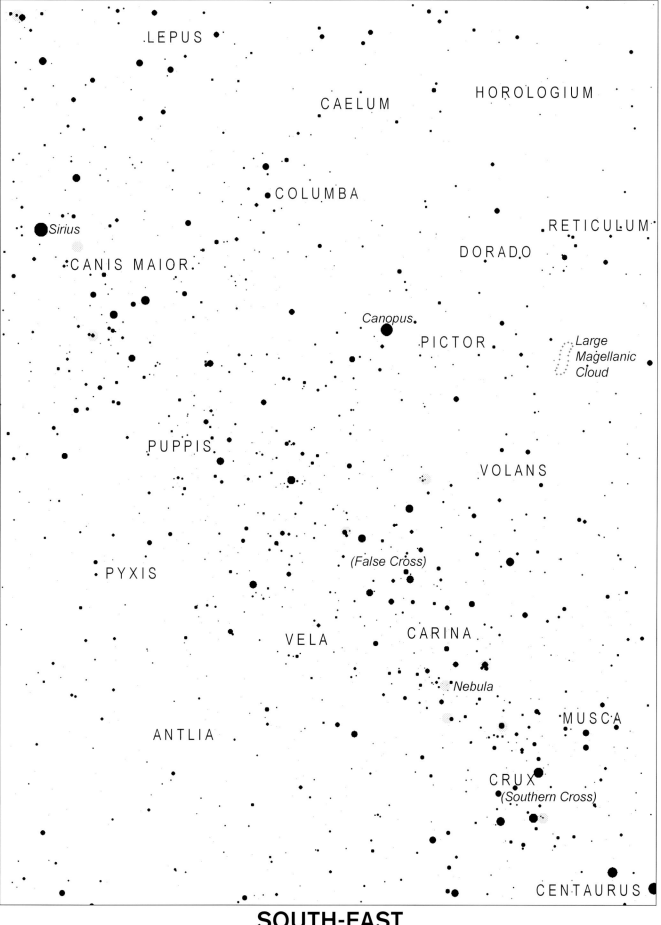

LEPUS

CAELUM

HOROLOGIUM

COLUMBA

Sirius

CANIS MAIOR.

RETICULUM

DORADO

Canopus.

PICTOR

*Large
Magellanic
Cloud*

PUPPIS

VOLANS

(False Cross)

PYXIS

VELA

CARINA

Nebula

MUSCA

ANTLIA

CRUX
(Southern Cross)

CENTAURUS

SOUTH-EAST

SEPTEMBER		OCTOBER	NOVEMBER	DECEMBER	**JANUARY**	
06h	05h	04h	03h	02h	01h	00h	23h	22h	**21h**	20h

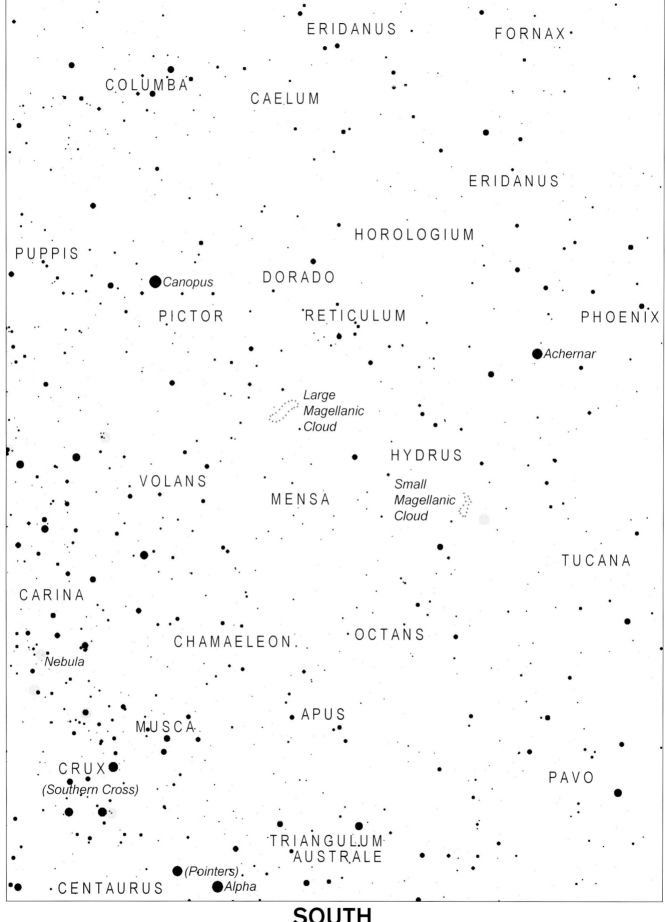

ERIDANUS   FORNAX

COLUMBA   CAELUM

ERIDANUS

HOROLOGIUM

PUPPIS

●*Canopus*   DORADO

PICTOR   RETICULUM   PHOENIX

●*Achernar*

Large Magellanic Cloud

HYDRUS

VOLANS   *Small Magellanic Cloud*

MENSA

TUCANA

CARINA

CHAMAELEON   OCTANS

Nebula

APUS

MUSCA

CRUX   PAVO
(Southern Cross)

TRIANGULUM AUSTRALE

(Pointers)

CENTAURUS   *Alpha*

SOUTH

| | SEPTEMBER | | OCTOBER | | NOVEMBER | | DECEMBER | | **JANUARY** | |
| 06h | | 05h | | 04h | 03h | 02h | 01h | 00h | 23h | 22h | **21h** | 20h |

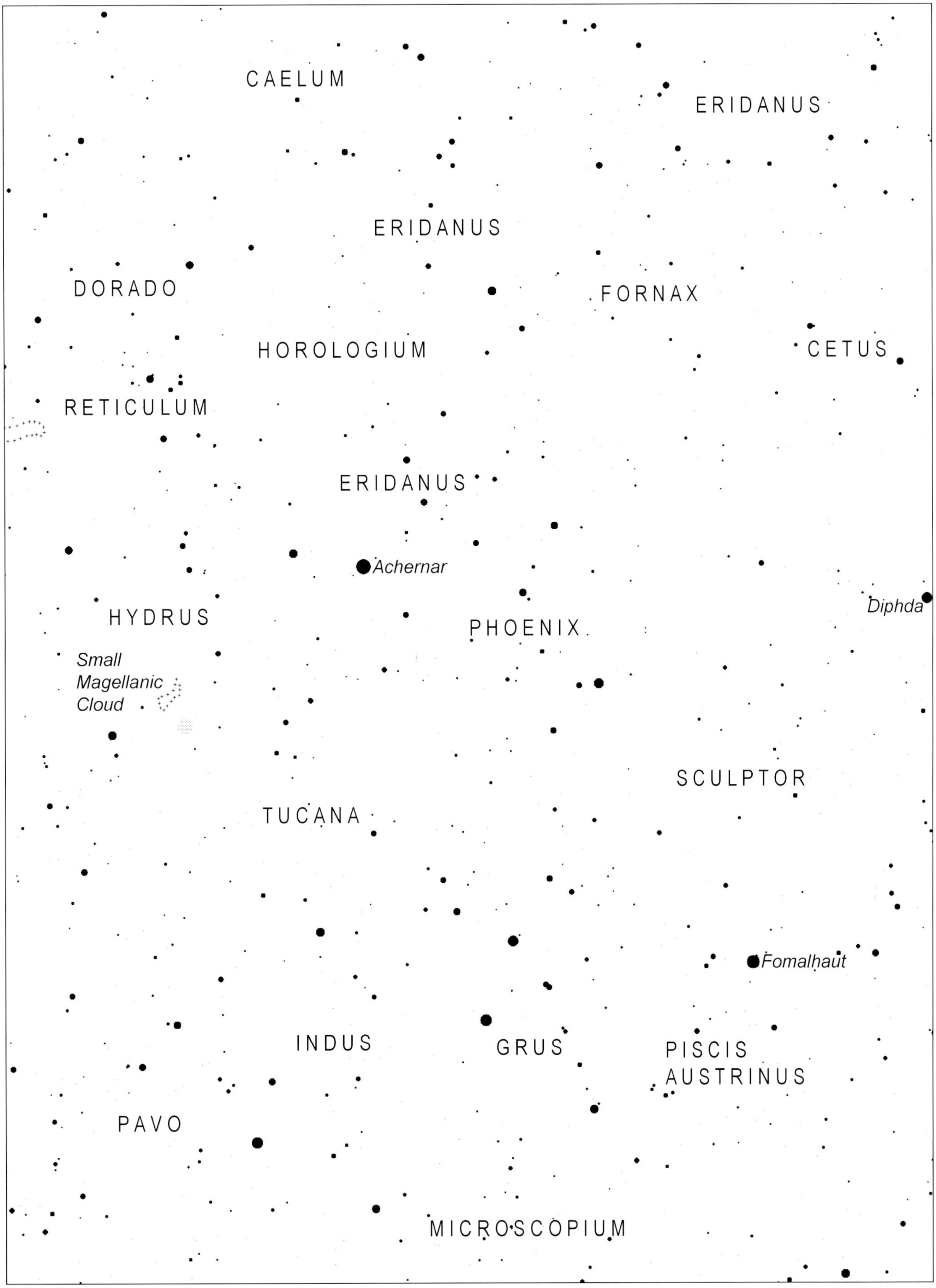

CAELUM

ERIDANUS

ERIDANUS

DORADO

FORNAX

HOROLOGIUM

CETUS

RETICULUM

ERIDANUS

●Achernar

Diphda

HYDRUS

PHOENIX

Small
Magellanic
Cloud

SCULPTOR

TUCANA

●Fomalhaut

INDUS

GRUS

PISCIS
AUSTRINUS

PAVO

MICROSCOPIUM

SOUTH-WEST

	SEPTEMBER		OCTOBER		NOVEMBER		DECEMBER		**JANUARY**	
06h	05h	04h	03h	02h	01h	00h	23h	22h	**21h**	20h

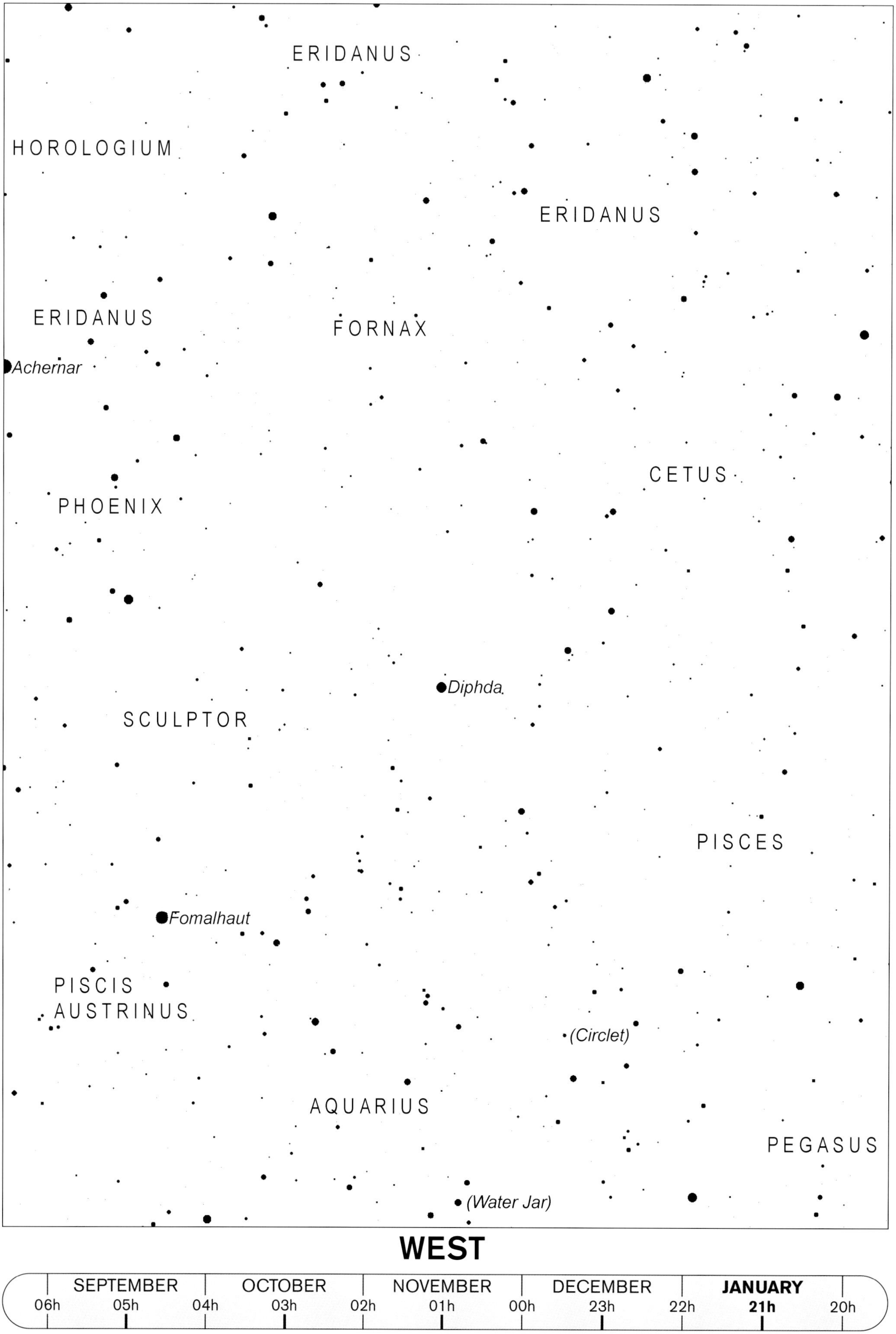

ERIDANUS

HOROLOGIUM

ERIDANUS

ERIDANUS

FORNAX

●Achernar

CETUS

PHOENIX

SCULPTOR

●Diphda

PISCES

●Fomalhaut

PISCIS
AUSTRINUS

(Circlet)

AQUARIUS

PEGASUS

(Water Jar)

WEST

SEPTEMBER		OCTOBER		NOVEMBER		DECEMBER		JANUARY	
06h	05h	04h	03h	02h	01h	00h	23h	22h	21h	20h

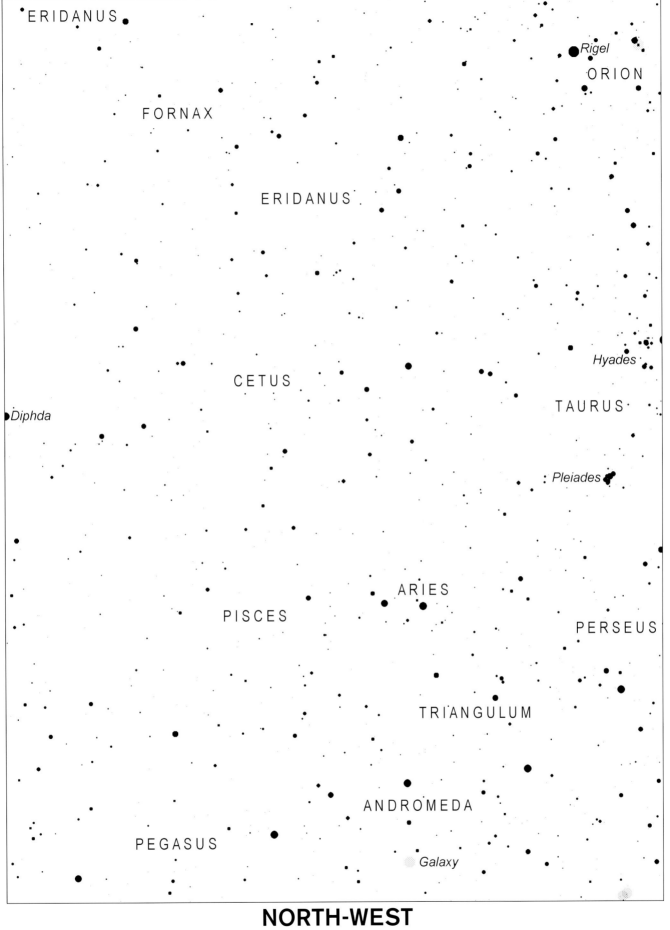

ERIDANUS

Rigel

ORION

FORNAX

ERIDANUS

Hyades

CETUS

TAURUS

Diphda

Pleiades

ARIES

PISCES

PERSEUS

TRIANGULUM

ANDROMEDA

PEGASUS

Galaxy

NORTH-WEST

SEPTEMBER	OCTOBER	NOVEMBER	DECEMBER	JANUARY	
06h 05h 04h	03h 02h	01h 00h	23h 22h	**21h**	20h

SET 2
FEBRUARY AT 21H
USE ALSO IN JANUARY AT 23H, DECEMBER AT 01H, NOVEMBER AT 03H, OCTOBER AT 05H

AT OTHER TIMES OF THE NIGHT IN **FEBRUARY,** USE: **SET 3** AT 23H, **SET 4** AT 01H, AND **SET 5** AT 03H

HIGHLIGHT OF THE SKY TONIGHT

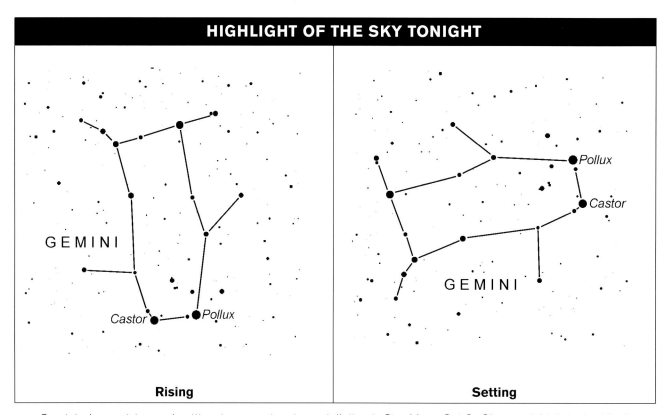

Rising   **Setting**

Gemini, shown rising and setting, is a prominent constellation in Star Maps Set 2. *Observe it high in the North.*

A guided tour of the sky

Due **North** there are many bright stars that form the huge Summer Hexagon. Starting from low-lying Capella in the constellation Auriga and, turning clockwise, you can find Aldebaran in Taurus, Rigel in Orion, Sirius in Canis Maior, Procyon in Canis Minor and the Twins, Castor and Pollux, in Gemini. The brightest star (after the Sun) – Sirius – is very high, and is almost directly above. Somewhat lower, the constellation of Orion is prominent, in which hot Rigel is bluish and cool Betelgeuse is red. You can see Orion's Belt (three stars in a row) and Orion's famous Nebula, using binoculars if necessary.

Cancer is difficult to identify in the **North-East**. Leo's Sickle is much easier to see, with Regulus as its handle.

The extended constellation, Hydra (the Water Snake), lies in the **East**. It contains only one rather bright star, Alphard. Near the horizon, you can see little Corvus – it looks quite striking.

Looking **South-East** you can see crowds of bright stars, all arranged along the Milky Way. The Pointer stars are very low. Alpha Centauri and Beta Centauri are referred to as the Pointers because they help us to locate tiny Crux or the Southern Cross constellation, higher up. A little higher again is Carina with its beautiful

Nebula or gas cloud. Still higher is the False Cross, which at first sight could be confused with the real Southern Cross despite the big differences between them.

Bright Canopus shines very high in the **South**. Below it, you can see both Magellanic Clouds, which are dwarf galaxies just beyond our own. These neighbouring galaxies are so far away that their light has travelled roughly two thousand centuries to reach us, whereas sunlight takes just over eight minutes to reach us. Use binoculars to view details in the Clouds. Do not expect to see individual stars – for this you need a telescope.

In the **South-West**, a bright star, Achernar, marks one end of the 'river' Eridanus (the other end is near the blue star, Rigel, in Orion). To the right of Achernar, our view is perpendicular to the Milky Way. The sky is almost empty there, indicating that our galaxy is not a sphere, but a flattened disk (like many other galaxies).

The sky in the **West** is dominated by the meandering 'river' Eridanus and the constellation of Cetus. Both are large, but are not easy to identify because they lack really bright stars. Diphda in Cetus is the brightest star in this part of the sky.

Two bright clusters are visible in the **North-West**. To the left of Aldebaran is an 'A'-shaped cluster called the Hyades. Just below it, you can find another one, the Pleiades (the Seven Sisters). Use binoculars for a wonderful view of these two clusters.

The Large Magellanic Cloud

Southern Cross versus False Cross

The so-called False Cross is not a real constellation: one half of it belongs to Vela, and the other half is part of Carina. It is said to mimic Crux, the Southern Cross. However, the False Cross is somewhat bigger than tiny Crux and its four stars are almost equal in brightness. Moreover, the False Cross lacks the distinctive Pointer stars that easily identify the real Southern Cross.

NEW MOON IN FEBRUARY

The week around new Moon is ideal for stargazing. A February new Moon will occur:

Year	Day	Year	Day
2004	20th	2014	*
2005	9th	2015	19th
2006	28th	2016	8th
2007	17th	2017	26th
2008	7th	2018	15th
2009	25th	2019	4th
2010	14th	2020	23rd
2011	3rd	2021	11th
2012	22nd	2022	1st
2013	10th		

*There will be no new Moon in February 2014. Please refer to January and March 2014.

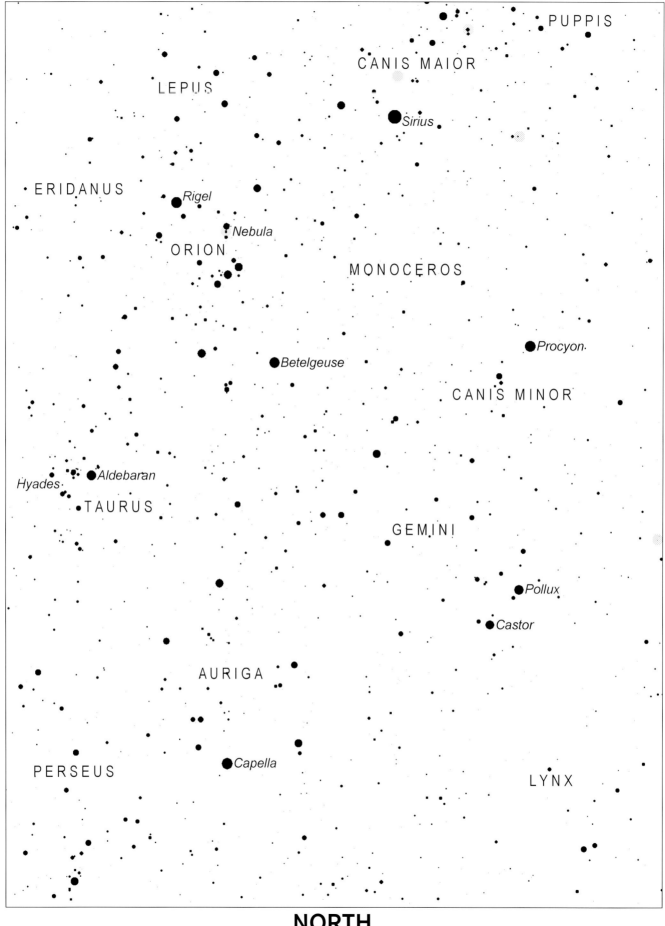

PUPPIS

CANIS MAIOR

LEPUS

● *Sirius*

ERIDANUS

● *Rigel*

● *Nebula*

ORION

MONOCEROS

● *Procyon*

CANIS MINOR

● *Betelgeuse*

Hyades ● *Aldebaran*

TAURUS

GEMINI

● *Pollux*

● *Castor*

AURIGA

PERSEUS

● *Capella*

LYNX

NORTH

	OCTOBER		NOVEMBER		DECEMBER		JANUARY		**FEBRUARY**	
06h	05h	04h	03h	02h	01h	00h	23h	22h	**21h**	20h

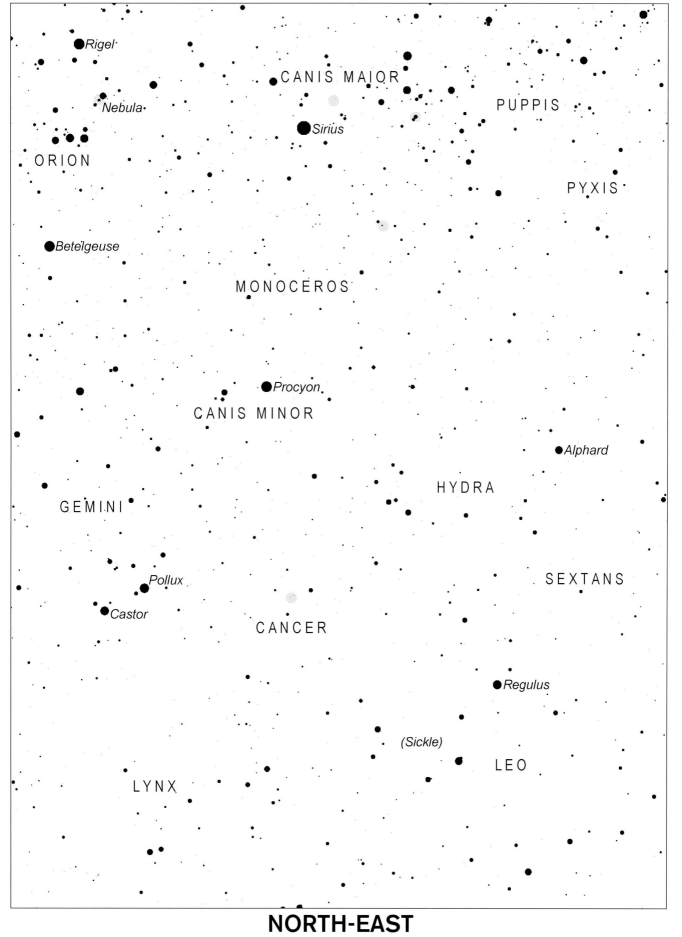

Rigel

CANIS MAJOR

PUPPIS

Nebula

Sirius

ORION

PYXIS

Betelgeuse

MONOCEROS

Procyon

CANIS MINOR

Alphard

HYDRA

GEMINI

SEXTANS

Pollux

Castor

CANCER

Regulus

(Sickle)

LYNX

LEO

NORTH-EAST

| | OCTOBER | | NOVEMBER | | DECEMBER | | JANUARY | | **FEBRUARY** | |
| 06h | 05h | 04h | 03h | 02h | 01h | 00h | 23h | 22h | **21h** | 20h |

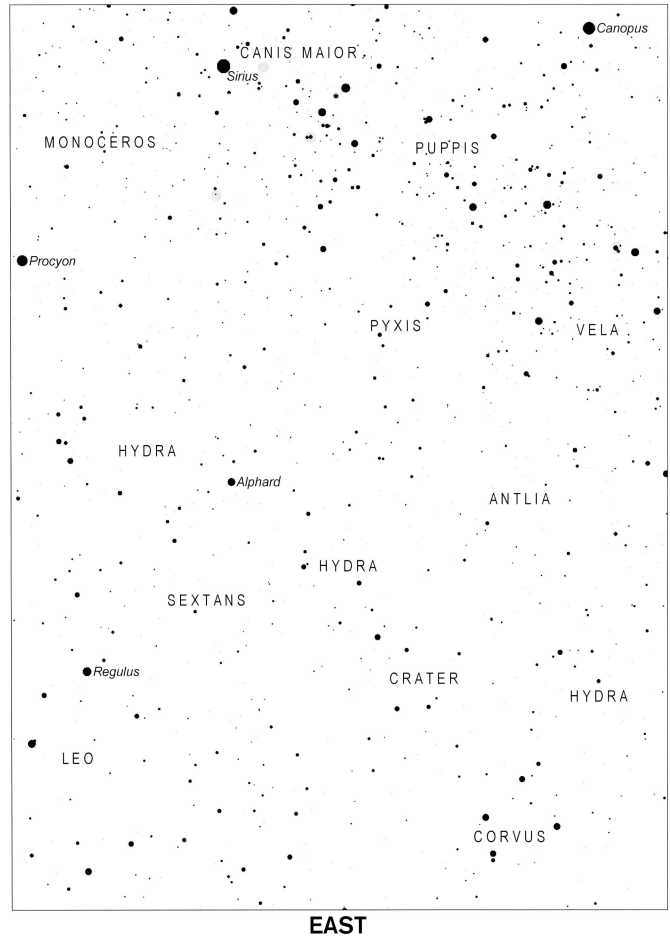

Canopus

CANIS MAIOR

Sirius

MONOCEROS

PUPPIS

Procyon

PYXIS

VELA

HYDRA

Alphard

ANTLIA

HYDRA

SEXTANS

Regulus

CRATER

HYDRA

LEO

CORVUS

EAST

OCTOBER	NOVEMBER	DECEMBER	JANUARY	FEBRUARY	
06h 05h	04h 03h	02h 01h	00h 23h	22h **21h**	20h

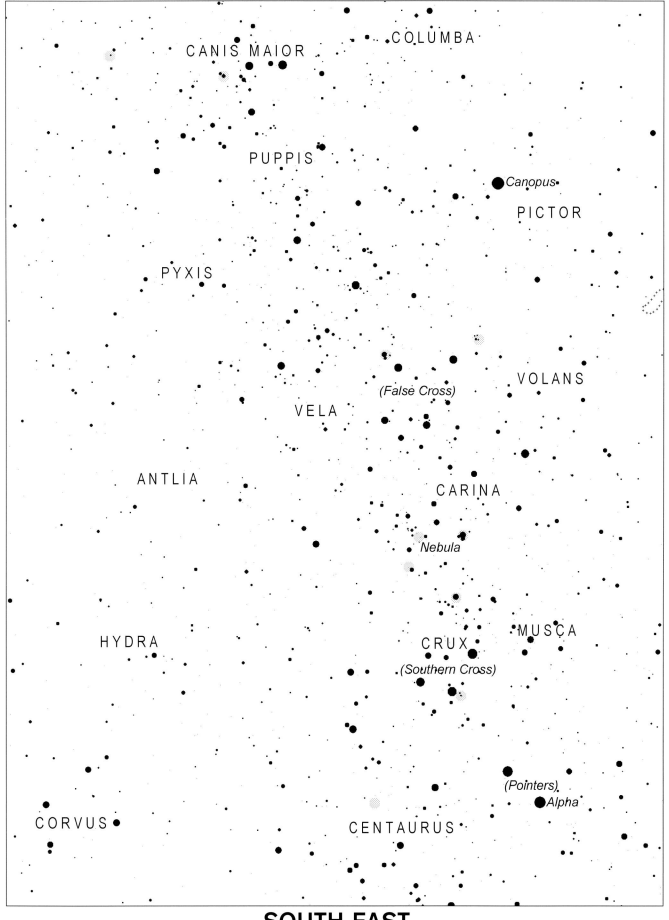

COLUMBA

CANIS MAIOR

PUPPIS

Canopus

PICTOR

PYXIS

VOLANS

(False Cross)

VELA

ANTLIA

CARINA

Nebula

MUSCA

HYDRA

CRUX

(Southern Cross)

(Pointers)

CORVUS

CENTAURUS

● *Alpha*

SOUTH-EAST

	OCTOBER	NOVEMBER	DECEMBER	JANUARY	FEBRUARY	
06h	05h	04h	03h	02h	01h	00h	23h	22h	**21h**	20h

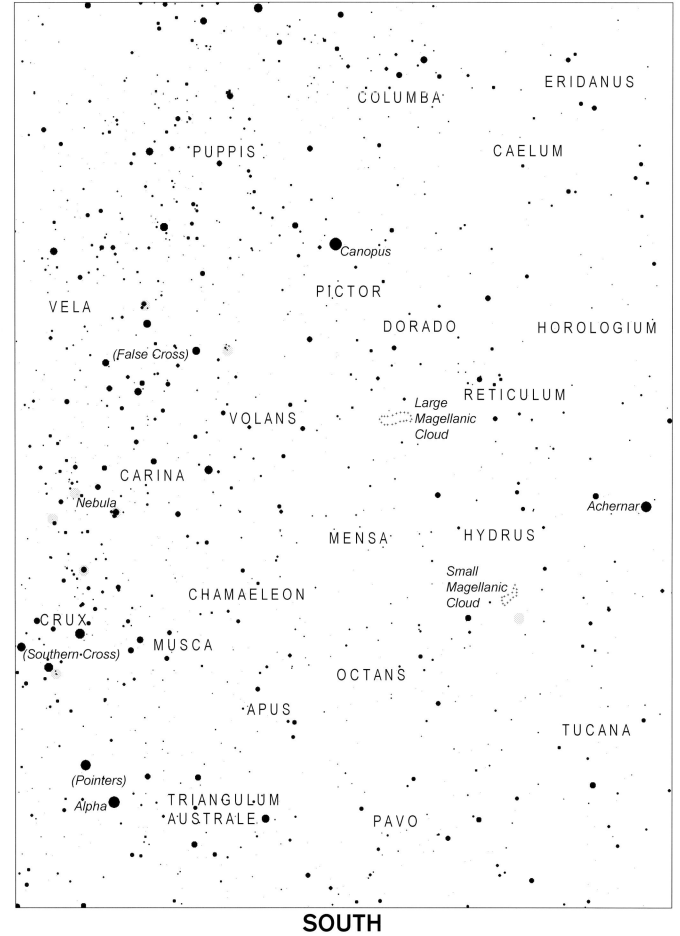

ERIDANUS

COLUMBA

CAELUM

PUPPIS

Canopus

PICTOR

VELA

DORADO   HOROLOGIUM

(False Cross)

RETICULUM

VOLANS

Large
Magellanic
Cloud

CARINA

Nebula

Achernar

MENSA   HYDRUS

CHAMAELEON

Small
Magellanic
Cloud

CRUX

(Southern·Cross)   MUSCA

OCTANS

APUS

TUCANA

(Pointers)

Alpha   TRIANGULUM
           AUSTRALE   PAVO

SOUTH

	OCTOBER	NOVEMBER	DECEMBER	JANUARY	**FEBRUARY**	
06h	05h	04h	03h	02h	01h	00h	23h	22h	**21h**	20h

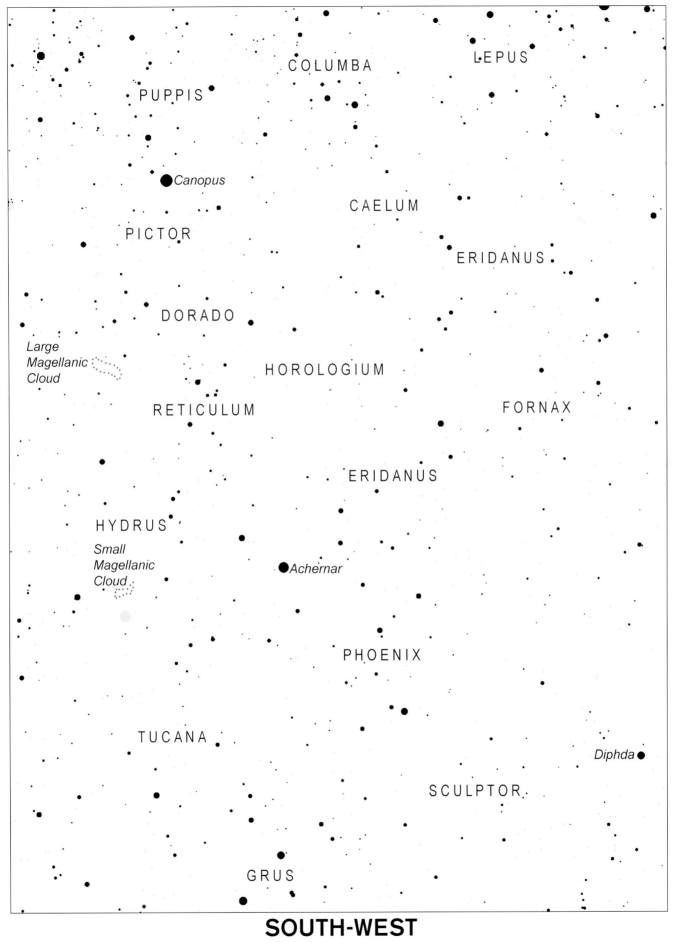

LEPUS

COLUMBA

PUPPIS

Canopus

CAELUM

PICTOR

ERIDANUS

DORADO

*Large
Magellanic
Cloud*

HOROLOGIUM

RETICULUM

FORNAX

ERIDANUS

HYDRUS

*Small
Magellanic
Cloud*

Achernar

PHOENIX

TUCANA

Diphda

SCULPTOR

GRUS

SOUTH-WEST

OCTOBER	NOVEMBER	DECEMBER	JANUARY	**FEBRUARY**	
06h	05h	04h	03h	02h	01h	00h	23h	22h	**21h**	20h

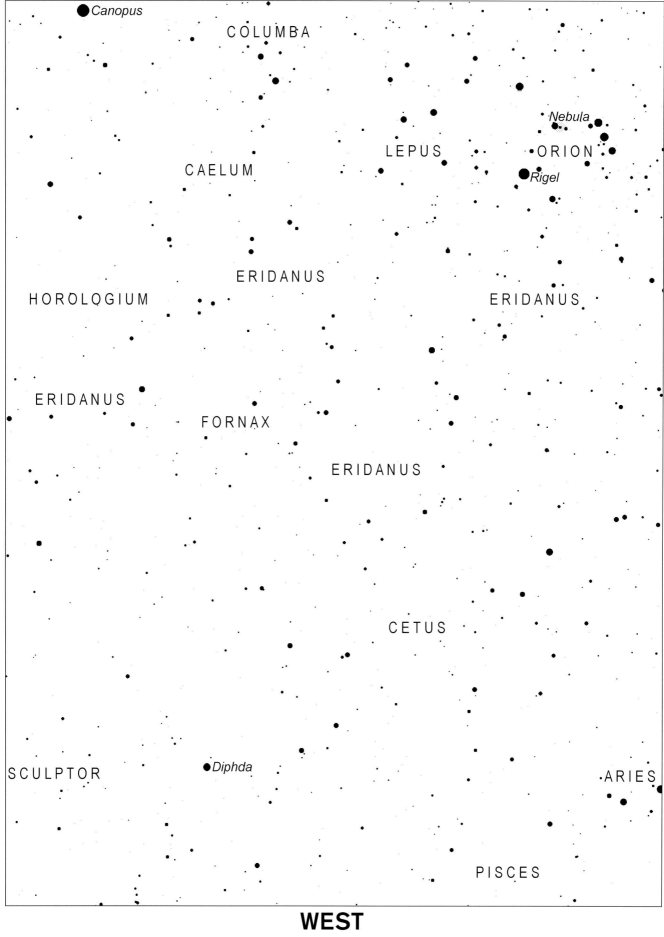

Canopus

COLUMBA

LEPUS

Nebula

ORION

CAELUM

Rigel

ERIDANUS

HOROLOGIUM

ERIDANUS

ERIDANUS

FORNAX

ERIDANUS

CETUS

SCULPTOR

Diphda

ARIES

PISCES

WEST

OCTOBER	NOVEMBER	DECEMBER	JANUARY	FEBRUARY	
06h 05h 04h	03h 02h	01h 00h	23h 22h	**21h**	20h

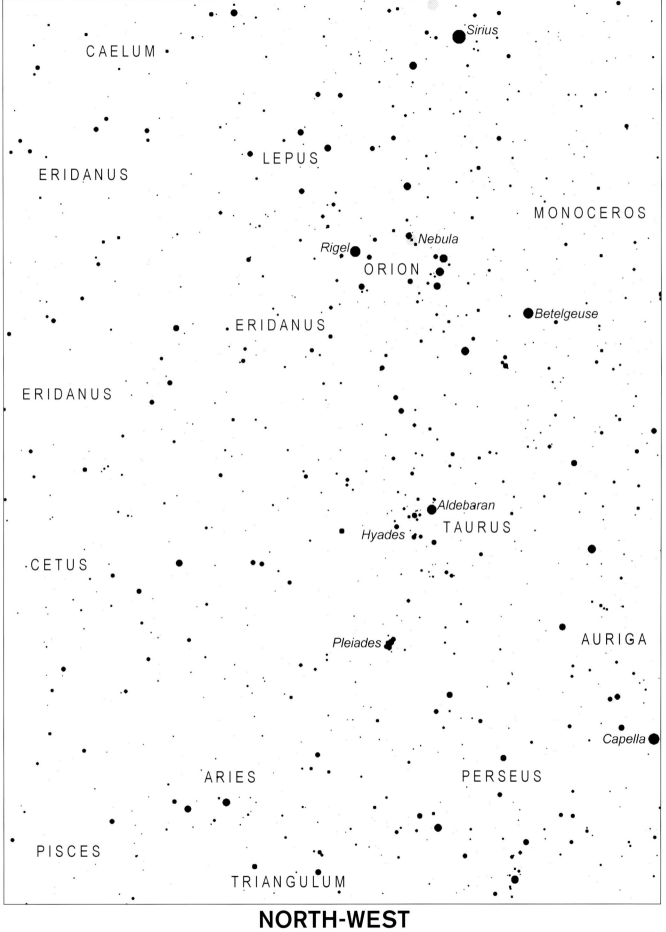

CAELUM

Sirius

ERIDANUS

LEPUS

MONOCEROS

Nebula

Rigel

ORION

ERIDANUS

Betelgeuse

ERIDANUS

Aldebaran

Hyades

TAURUS

CETUS

AURIGA

Pleiades

Capella

ARIES

PERSEUS

PISCES

TRIANGULUM

NORTH-WEST

OCTOBER		NOVEMBER		DECEMBER		JANUARY		**FEBRUARY**	
06h	05h	04h	03h	02h	01h	00h	23h	22h	**21h**	20h

SET 3

MARCH AT 21H

USE ALSO IN APRIL AT 19H, FEBRUARY AT 23H, JANUARY AT 01H, DECEMBER AT 03H

AT OTHER TIMES IN MARCH, USE: SET 4 AT 23H, SET 5 AT 01H, SET 6 AT 03H, AND SET 7 AT 05H

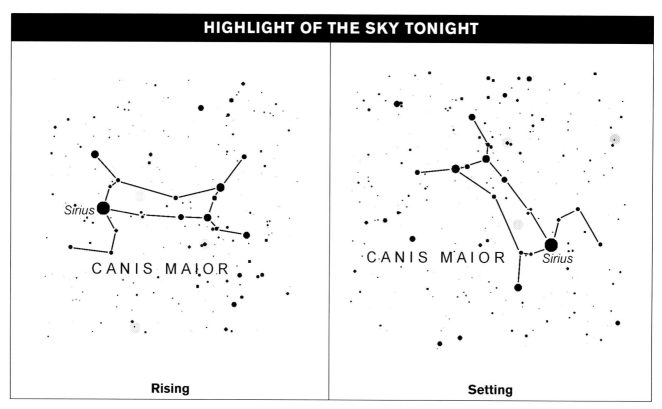

HIGHLIGHT OF THE SKY TONIGHT

Rising

Setting

Canis Maior, shown rising and setting, is a prominent constellation in Star Maps Set 3. *Observe it very high in the West.*

A guided tour of the sky

Looking towards the **North**, you can see the Twins, Castor and Pollux, which are part of the constellation of Gemini. Higher up, Procyon is visible in the constellation of Canis Minor.

Leo's constellation is visible in the **North-East**. Look for Leo's Sickle, bright Regulus and Denebola. Much higher, you can find Alphard, the only bright star of the extended Hydra (the Water Snake) constellation.

In the **East** you can see the constellation of Virgo with its bright star, Spica. Above this star is little Corvus, a constellation that is striking in a dark expanse of sky.

Many bright stars are visible in the **South-East**. Most of them appear to be lined up along the Milky Way. The constellation of Centaurus is rather low, but its Pointers are obvious. Alpha Centauri is our nearest star, after the Sun. Its light has travelled for more than four years to reach us. Somewhat higher is Crux. A dark cloud of interstellar dust can be seen immediately below Crux. Higher up is Carina with its beautiful Nebula, visible to the naked eye. Use binoculars to see the detail.

Still higher, and further **South**, is the False Cross, which is said to mimic the smaller Southern Cross constellation. Nevertheless, there are obvious differences.

Lower in the sky is the Large Magellanic Cloud, and still lower, the Small Cloud. These dwarf galaxies lie just outside the one we live in and are easily visible to the naked eye. Their light takes roughly two thousand centuries to reach us.

Bright Canopus is high up in the **South-West**. Canopus forms an outlying part of the Carina constellation. Achernar (the bright star at one end of Eridanus) shines below.

High in the **West** Canis Maior is visible. Its brilliant star, Sirius, is the brightest one in the sky, apart from our Sun. The lower half of the western sky is dominated by the meandering 'river' constellation, Eridanus, which ends near the star Rigel in Orion.

In the **North-West** you can see the 'Summer Hexagon'. Capella, a star in the constellation of Auriga is near the horizon. Turning clockwise, you can find the following stars: Aldebaran in the constellation of Taurus; Rigel in Orion; Sirius in Canis Maior; Procyon in Canis Minor, and the Twin stars, Castor and Pollux, in Gemini. Orion is the most prominent constellation. Look for its Belt (three stars in a row) and Nebula, from which new stars are forming. See the striking colour contrast between cool, red Betelgeuse and hot, blue Rigel, using binoculars.

Orion's Nebula (top) and Orion's Belt (bottom)

Constellations

Stars in a constellation are often at widely varying distances. They are not related in space but, seen from Earth, appear to lie along the same line of sight. Constellations are used to indicate positions of stars in the sky, but are not physical entities. Different cultures have created different constellations. Those used in this book are among the 88 that were officially recognized in 1928 by the International Astronomical Union (IAU).

NEW MOON IN MARCH

The week around new Moon is ideal for stargazing. A March new Moon will occur:

Year	Day	Year	Day
2004	21st	2014	1st & 30th
2005	10th	2015	20th
2006	29th	2016	9th
2007	19th	2017	28th
2008	7th	2018	17th
2009	26th	2019	6th
2010	15th	2020	24th
2011	4th	2021	13th
2012	22nd	2022	2nd
2013	11th		

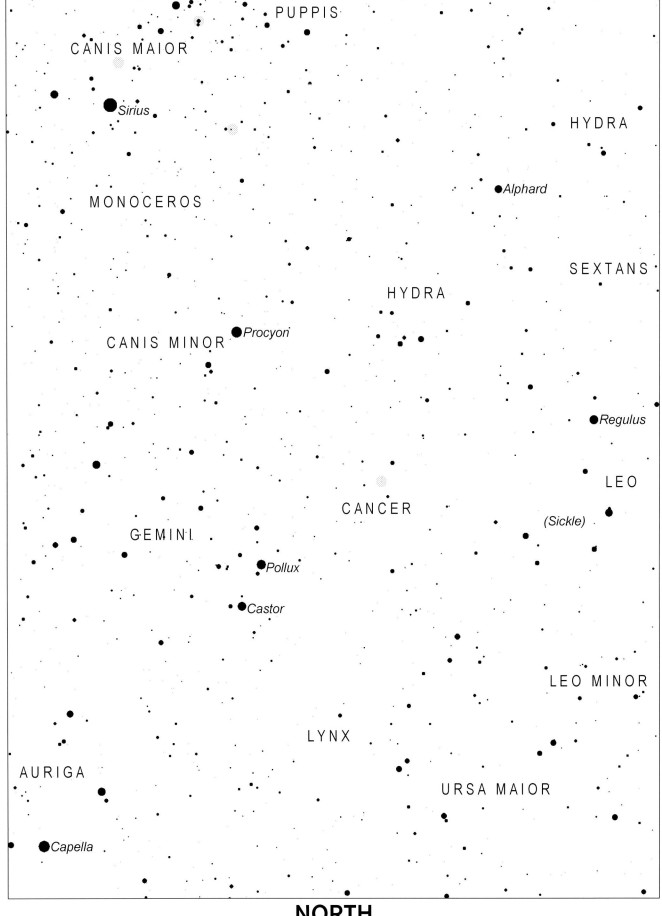

PUPPIS

CANIS MAIOR

Sirius

HYDRA

Alphard

MONOCEROS

SEXTANS

HYDRA

CANIS MINOR   Procyon

Regulus

LEO

CANCER

(Sickle)

GEMINI

Pollux

Castor

LEO MINOR

LYNX

AURIGA

URSA MAIOR

Capella

NORTH

DECEMBER		JANUARY		FEBRUARY			**MARCH**		APRIL	
04h	03h	02h	01h	00h	23h	22h	**21h**	20h	19h	18h

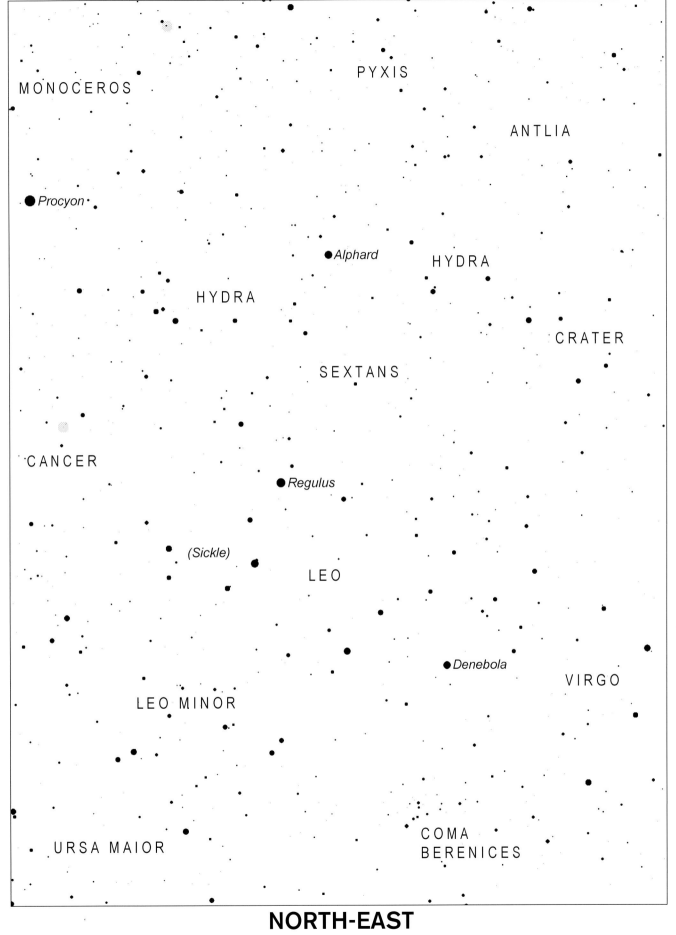

MONOCEROS

PYXIS

ANTLIA

● *Procyon*

● *Alphard*

HYDRA

HYDRA

CRATER

SEXTANS

CANCER

● *Regulus*

(Sickle)

LEO

● *Denebola*

VIRGO

LEO MINOR

COMA
BERENICES

URSA MAIOR

NORTH-EAST

	DECEMBER		JANUARY		FEBRUARY		**MARCH**		APRIL	
04h	03h	02h	01h	00h	23h	22h	**21h**	20h	19h	18h

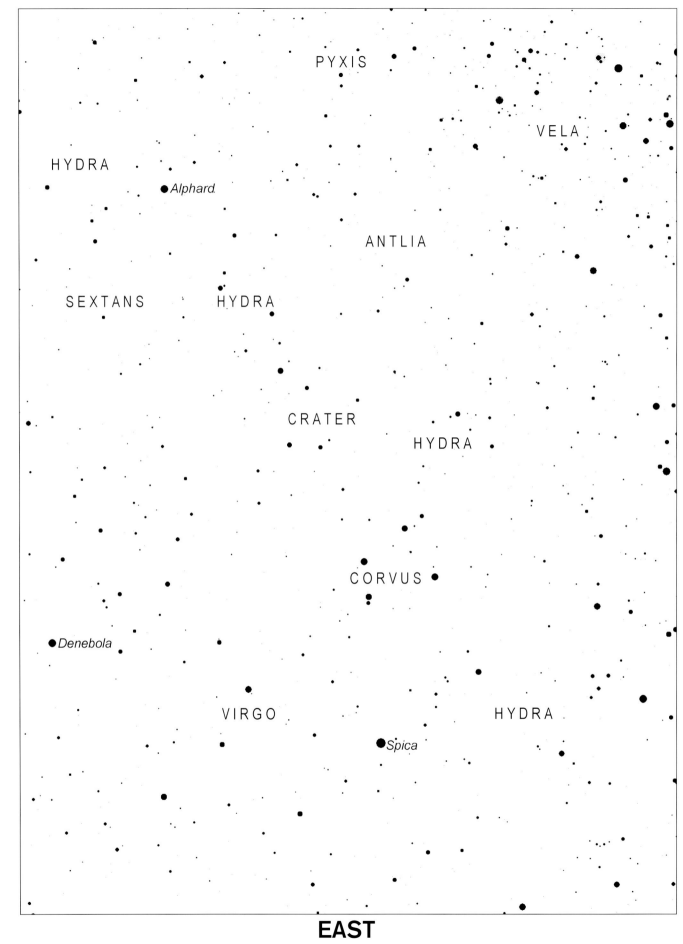

PYXIS

VELA

HYDRA

● *Alphard*

ANTLIA

SEXTANS   HYDRA

CRATER

HYDRA

CORVUS ●

● *Denebola*

VIRGO   HYDRA

● *Spica*

EAST

DECEMBER	JANUARY	FEBRUARY	**MARCH**	APRIL
04h 03h 02h	01h 00h	23h 22h	**21h** 20h	19h 18h

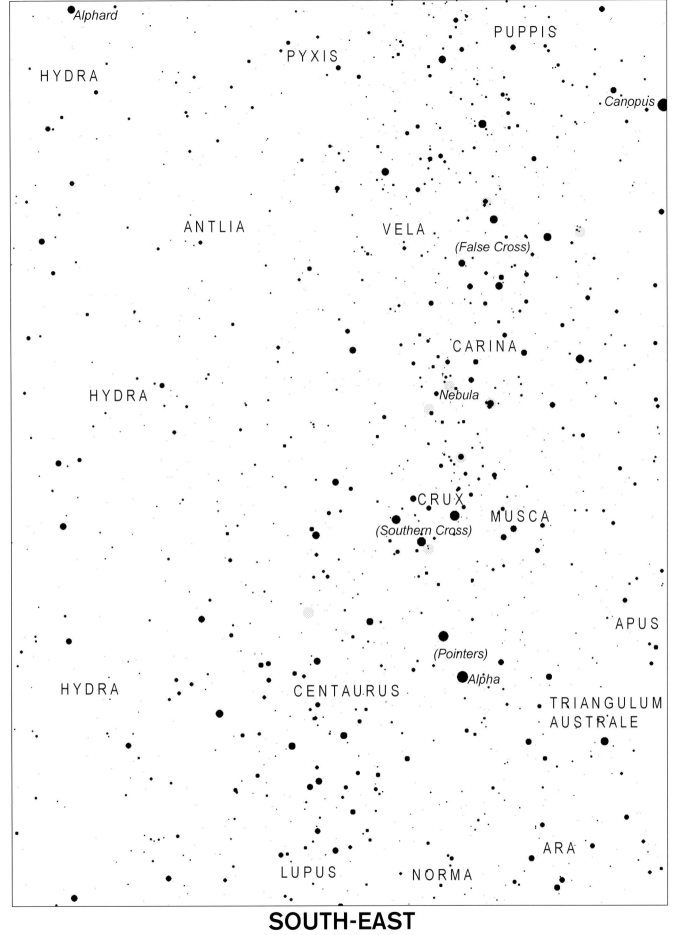

Alphard

PUPPIS

PYXIS

HYDRA

Canopus

ANTLIA

VELA

(False Cross)

CARINA

HYDRA

Nebula

CRUX

MUSCA

(Southern Cross)

APUS

(Pointers)

HYDRA

CENTAURUS

Alpha

TRIANGULUM
AUSTRALE

ARA

LUPUS

NORMA

SOUTH-EAST

	DECEMBER		JANUARY		FEBRUARY		MARCH		APRIL	
04h	03h	02h	01h	00h	23h	22h	**21h**	20h	19h	18h

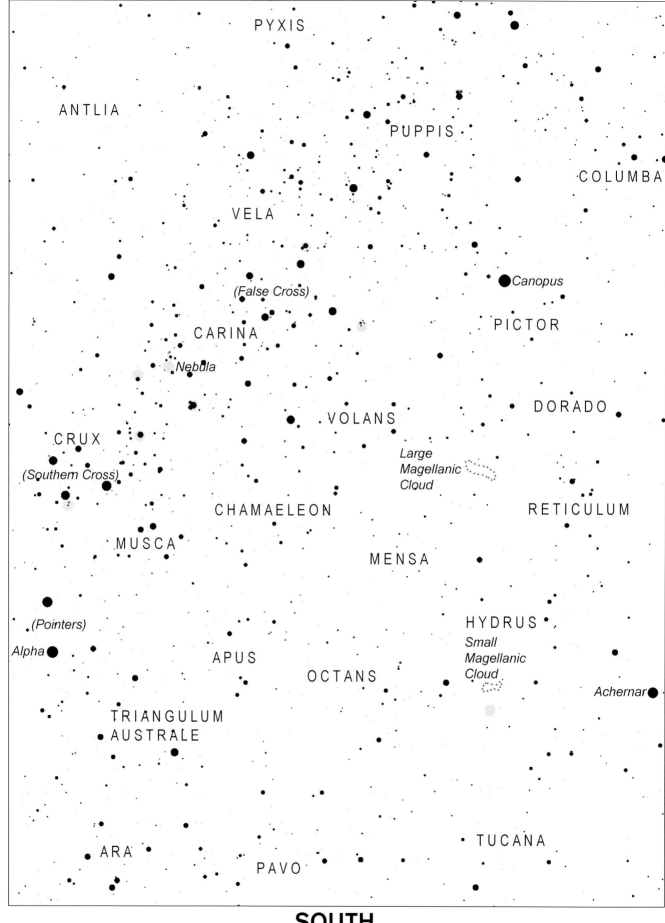

PYXIS

ANTLIA

PUPPIS

COLUMBA

VELA

Canopus

(False Cross)

PICTOR

CARINA

Nebula

DORADO

VOLANS

CRUX

Large
Magellanic
Cloud

RETICULUM

(Southern Cross)

CHAMAELEON

MUSCA

MENSA

(Pointers)

HYDRUS

Alpha

Small
Magellanic
Cloud

APUS

Achernar

OCTANS

TRIANGULUM
AUSTRALE

ARA

TUCANA

PAVO

SOUTH

DECEMBER		JANUARY		FEBRUARY			MARCH		APRIL	
04h	03h	02h	01h	00h	23h	22h	**21h**	20h	19h	18h

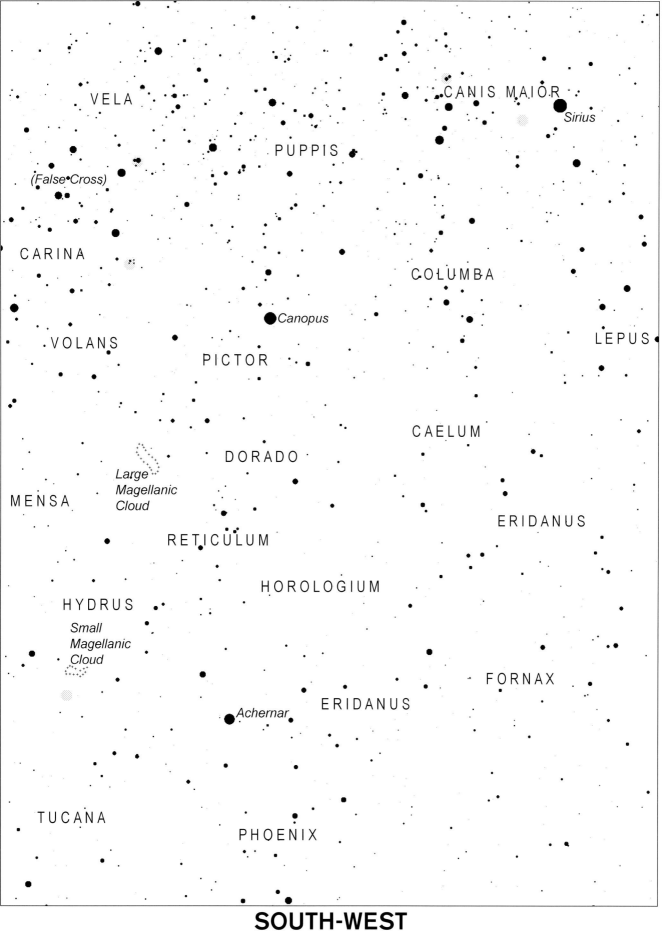

VELA

CANIS MAIOR

Sirius

PUPPIS

(False Cross)

CARINA

COLUMBA

Canopus

LEPUS

VOLANS

PICTOR

CAELUM

DORADO

Large Magellanic Cloud

MENSA

ERIDANUS

RETICULUM

HOROLOGIUM

HYDRUS

Small Magellanic Cloud

FORNAX

Achernar

ERIDANUS

TUCANA

PHOENIX

SOUTH-WEST

DECEMBER	JANUARY	FEBRUARY	**MARCH**	APRIL
04h 03h 02h	01h 00h	23h 22h	**21h** 20h	19h 18h

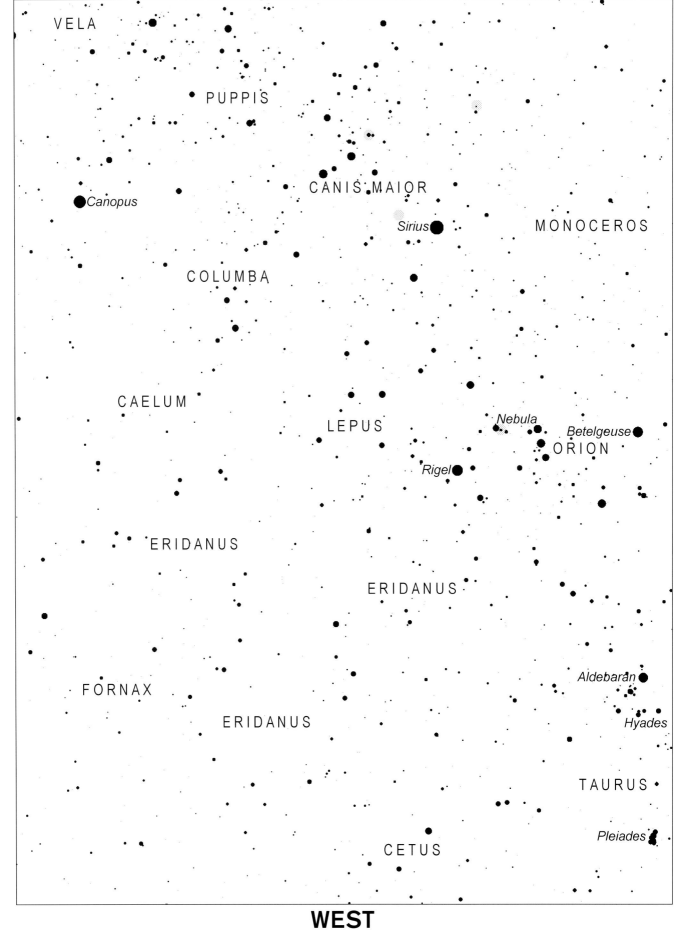

VELA

PUPPIS

CANIS MAIOR

●Canopus

Sirius●

MONOCEROS

COLUMBA

CAELUM

LEPUS

Nebula

Betelgeuse●

ORION

Rigel●

ERIDANUS

ERIDANUS

Aldebaran●

Hyades

FORNAX

ERIDANUS

TAURUS

Pleiades

CETUS

WEST

DECEMBER		JANUARY		FEBRUARY		**MARCH**		APRIL	
04h	03h	02h	01h	00h	23h	22h	**21h**	20h	19h	18h

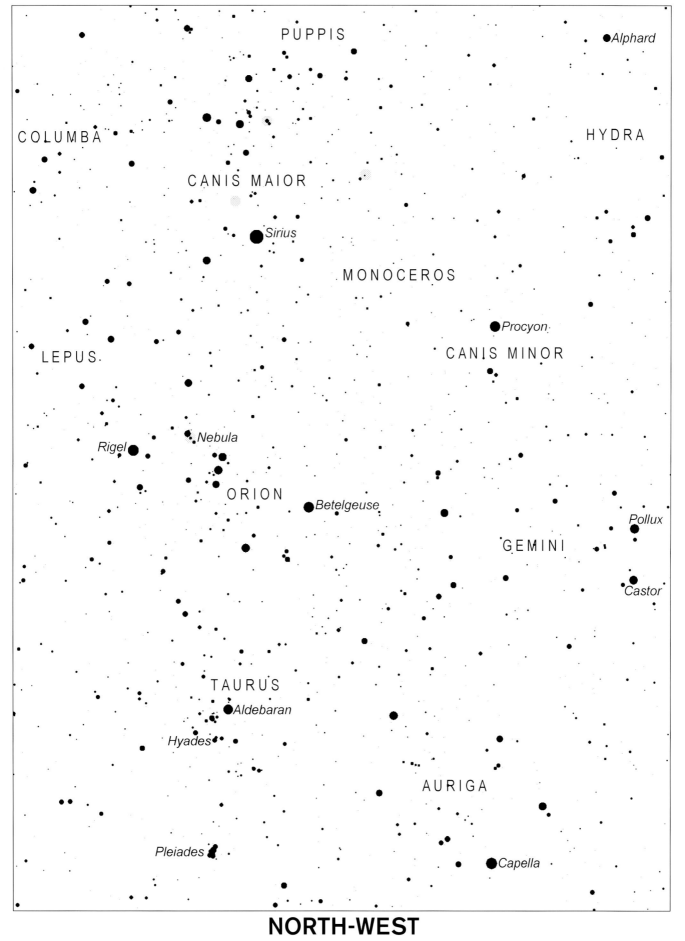

PUPPIS

COLUMBA

CANIS MAIOR

HYDRA

Alphard

Sirius

MONOCEROS

Procyon

CANIS MINOR

LEPUS

Nebula

Rigel

ORION

Betelgeuse

Pollux

GEMINI

Castor

TAURUS

Aldebaran

Hyades

AURIGA

Pleiades

Capella

NORTH-WEST

DECEMBER		JANUARY		FEBRUARY		**MARCH**		APRIL	
04h	03h	02h	01h	00h	23h	22h	**21h**	20h	19h	18h

SET 4
APRIL AT 21H

USE ALSO IN **MAY** AT 19H, **MARCH** AT 23H, **FEBRUARY** AT 01H, **JANUARY** AT 03H

AT OTHER TIMES IN **APRIL**, USE: **SET 3** AT 19H, **SET 5** AT 23H, **SET 6** AT 01H, **SET 7** AT 03H, **SET 8** AT 05H

HIGHLIGHT OF THE SKY TONIGHT

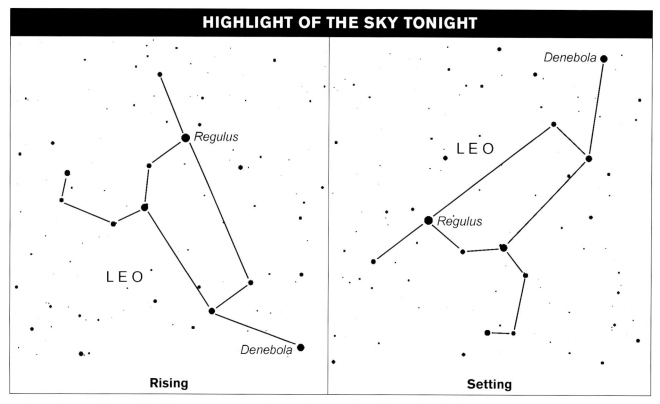

Rising   **Setting**

Leo, shown rising and setting, is a prominent constellation in Star Maps Set 4. *Observe it fairly high in the North.*

A guided tour of the sky

The constellation of Leo is high up in the **North**, with two bright stars, Regulus and Denebola. Regulus is the handle of the Sicklc.

Below Denebola and closer to the **North-East**, you can spot a large cluster named Coma Berenices. Use binoculars to see more detail. Bright Arcturus is a cool, orange star that can be seen low in the sky.

Bright Spica, in the constellation of Virgo, is visible high in the **East**. Two constellations are nearby: Corvus is just above Spica, and Libra is quite a distance below it and to the right.

Look for the giant constellation of Scorpius, towards the **South-East**. It is lying near the horizon. Antares is its brightest star and is red. Higher up along the Milky Way, you can see crowds of bright stars, of which a handful stand out clearly. The Pointers are high in the sky. They are the brightest pair of stars in Centaurus. One of the Pointers, Alpha Centauri, is our Sun's closest neighbour. Higher up you can see tiny Crux. It is the smallest constellation, but is extremely rich in stars. Standard 7 x 50 binoculars show how the whole constellation, visible in one view, teems with innumerable faint stars. It is an impressive sight.

Open clusters around the Carina Nebula

Carina is due **South**. Using binoculars, you will be able to see much detail in its beautiful Nebula. In 1843, a star exploded right within the Nebula and for several months it was brighter than Canopus. Today it is faint, but is the most studied star after the Sun and is likely to remain so. Further right is the so-called False Cross, not to be confused with the Southern Cross constellation. Much lower is the Large Magellanic Cloud, and still lower, the Small Magellanic Cloud.

Bright Canopus shines high in the **South-West**. Traditionally, this star is considered to be an outlying part of the constellation of Carina, and is its brightest star.

Sirius, the brightest star after the Sun, is visible due **West**. Sirius is sometimes called the Dog Star, for it is part of the constellation Canis Maior, the Big Dog. Far below, you shall soon bid farewell to Orion and its attendant Betelgeuse, Rigel, Belt and Nebula before they disappear from view.

Low in the **North-West** is Gemini, with its Twins, Castor and Pollux. Higher up in the sky, Procyon is visible in the constellation of Canis Minor, the Little Dog. The constellation of Cancer is situated to the right of Canis Minor, where keen eyes can spot a dim fuzziness, if the sky is dark enough. Using binoculars, you can see it is a cluster. Alphard is high up, and is the only conspicuous star in the constellation of Hydra.

The brightest stars in the sky

In southern Africa, in the first half of April, it is possible to spot the 33 brightest stars during *one single night*. In order to accomplish this, you need a very clear sky and a totally unobstructed view of the horizon in the North-West, North, and North-East. Use map Sets 3 to 8 in all directions.

NEW MOON IN APRIL

The week around new Moon is ideal for stargazing. An April new Moon will occur:

Year	Day	Year	Day
2004	19th	2014	29th
2005	8th	2015	18th
2006	27th	2016	7th
2007	17th	2017	26th
2008	6th	2018	16th
2009	25th	2019	5th
2010	14th	2020	23rd
2011	3rd	2021	12th
2012	21st	2022	1st & 30th
2013	10th		

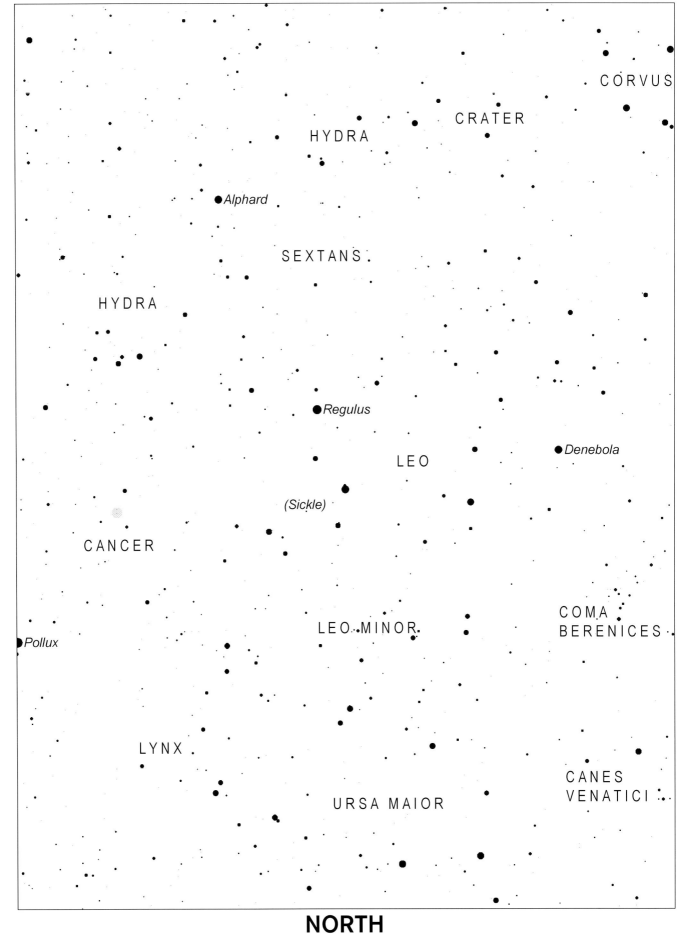

CORVUS

CRATER

HYDRA

●Alphard

SEXTANS

HYDRA

●Regulus

LEO

●Denebola

(Sickle)

CANCER

LEO MINOR

COMA
BERENICES

●Pollux

LYNX

CANES
VENATICI

URSA MAIOR

NORTH

	JANUARY	FEBRUARY	MARCH	**APRIL**	MAY	
04h	03h	02h 01h	00h 23h	22h **21h**	20h 19h	18h

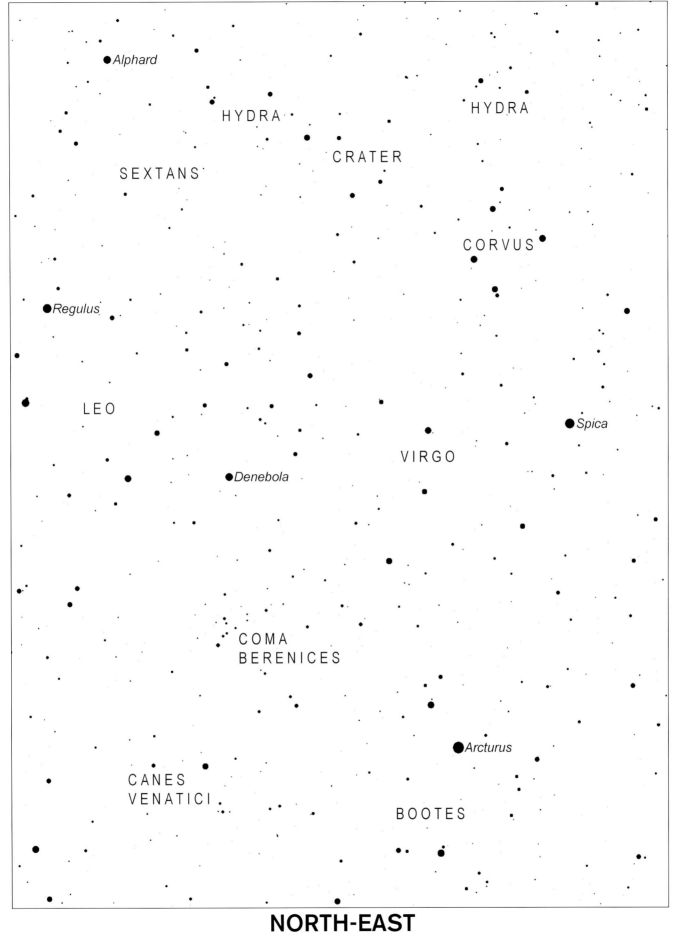

NORTH-EAST

	JANUARY		FEBRUARY		MARCH		**APRIL**		MAY	
04h	03h	02h	01h	00h	23h	22h	**21h**	20h	19h	18h

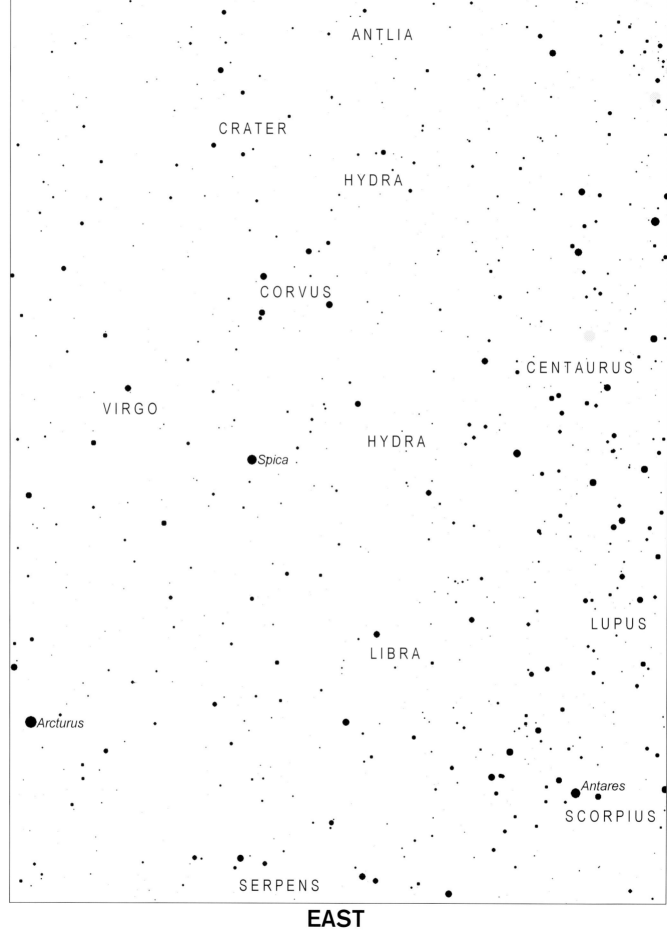

ANTLIA

CRATER

HYDRA

CORVUS

CENTAURUS

VIRGO

HYDRA

Spica

LUPUS

LIBRA

Arcturus

Antares

SCORPIUS

SERPENS

EAST

| | JANUARY | | FEBRUARY | | MARCH | | **APRIL** | | MAY | |
| 04h | 03h | 02h | 01h | 00h | 23h | 22h | **21h** | 20h | 19h | 18h |

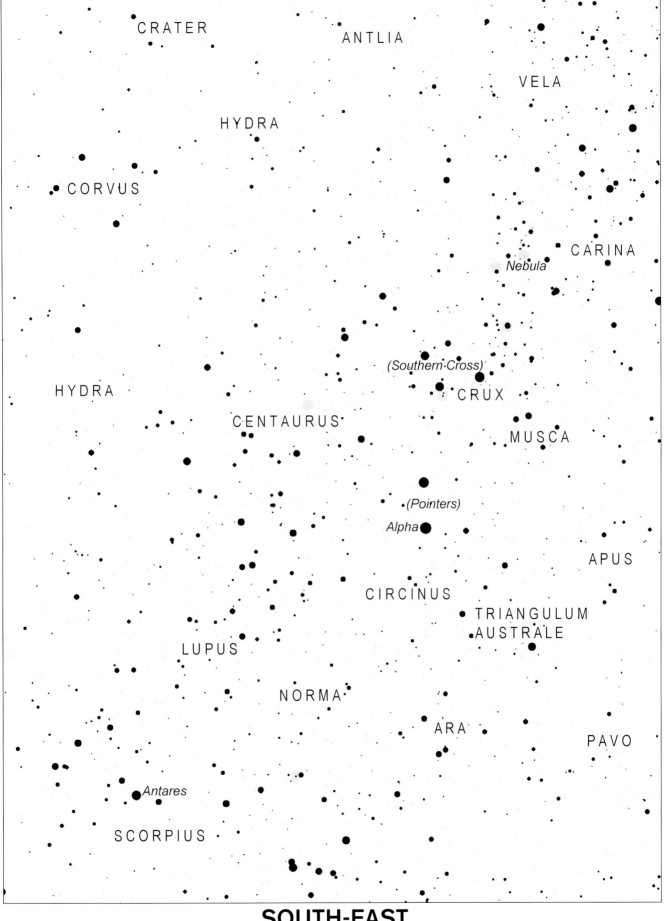

CRATER

ANTLIA

VELA

HYDRA

CARINA

CORVUS

Nebula

(Southern Cross)

CRUX

HYDRA

CENTAURUS

MUSCA

(Pointers)

APUS

Alpha

CIRCINUS

TRIANGULUM
AUSTRALE

LUPUS

NORMA

ARA

PAVO

Antares

SCORPIUS

SOUTH-EAST

JANUARY		FEBRUARY		MARCH			**APRIL**		MAY	
04h	03h	02h	01h	00h	23h	22h	**21h**	20h	19h	18h

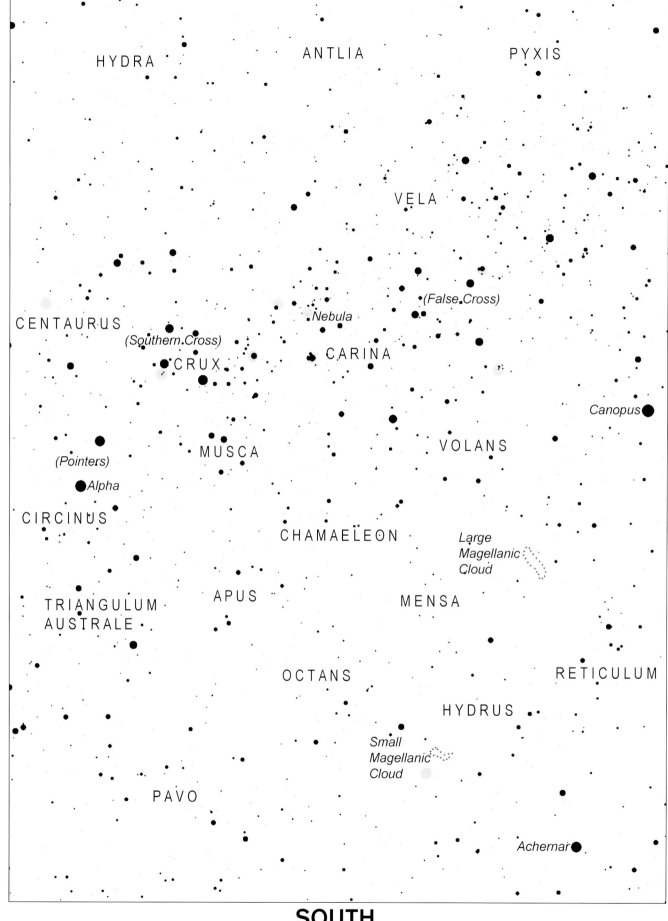

HYDRA

ANTLIA

PYXIS

VELA

(False Cross)

CENTAURUS

Nebula

(Southern Cross)

CARINA

CRUX

Canopus

MUSCA

VOLANS

(Pointers)

Alpha

CIRCINUS

CHAMAELEON

Large
Magellanic
Cloud

APUS

MENSA

TRIANGULUM
AUSTRALE

OCTANS

RETICULUM

HYDRUS

Small
Magellanic
Cloud

PAVO

Achernar

SOUTH

JANUARY	FEBRUARY	MARCH	**APRIL**	MAY
04h 03h 02h	01h 00h	23h 22h	**21h** 20h	19h 18h

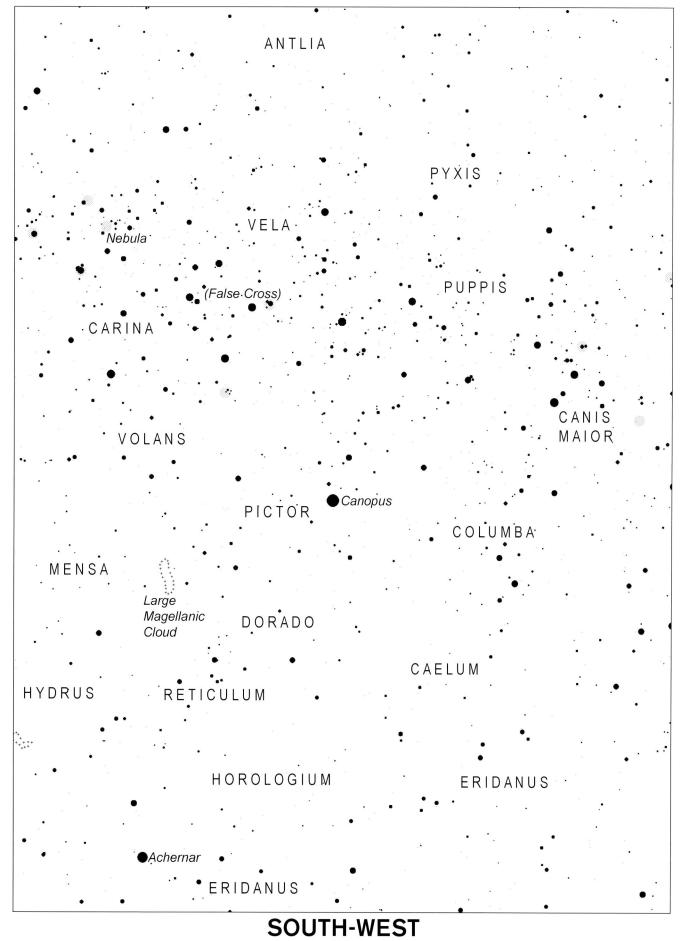

ANTLIA

PYXIS

VELA

Nebula

(False Cross)

PUPPIS

CARINA

CANIS
MAIOR

VOLANS

PICTOR ●*Canopus*

COLUMBA

MENSA

*Large
Magellanic
Cloud*

DORADO

CAELUM

HYDRUS

RETICULUM

HOROLOGIUM

ERIDANUS

●*Achernar*

ERIDANUS

SOUTH-WEST

JANUARY	FEBRUARY	MARCH	**APRIL**	MAY
04h 03h 02h	01h 00h	23h 22h	**21h** 20h	19h 18h

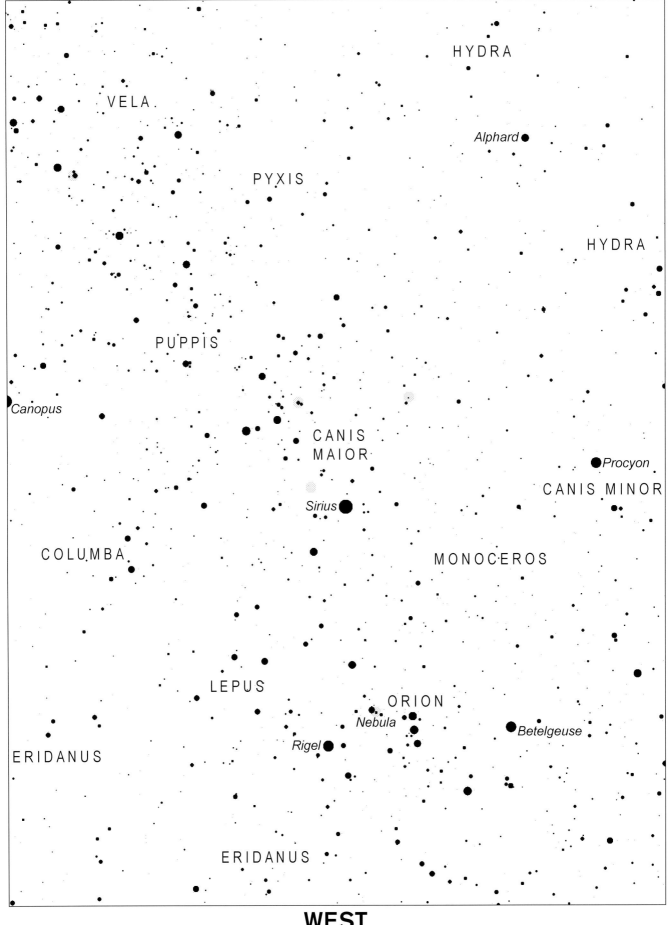

HYDRA

VELA

Alphard ●

PYXIS

HYDRA

PUPPIS

● *Canopus*

CANIS
MAIOR

● *Procyon*

CANIS MINOR

Sirius ●

COLUMBA

MONOCEROS

LEPUS

ORION

Betelgeuse

Nebula

ERIDANUS

Rigel

ERIDANUS

WEST

	JANUARY		FEBRUARY		MARCH		**APRIL**		MAY	
04h	03h	02h	01h	00h	23h	22h	**21h**	20h	19h	18h

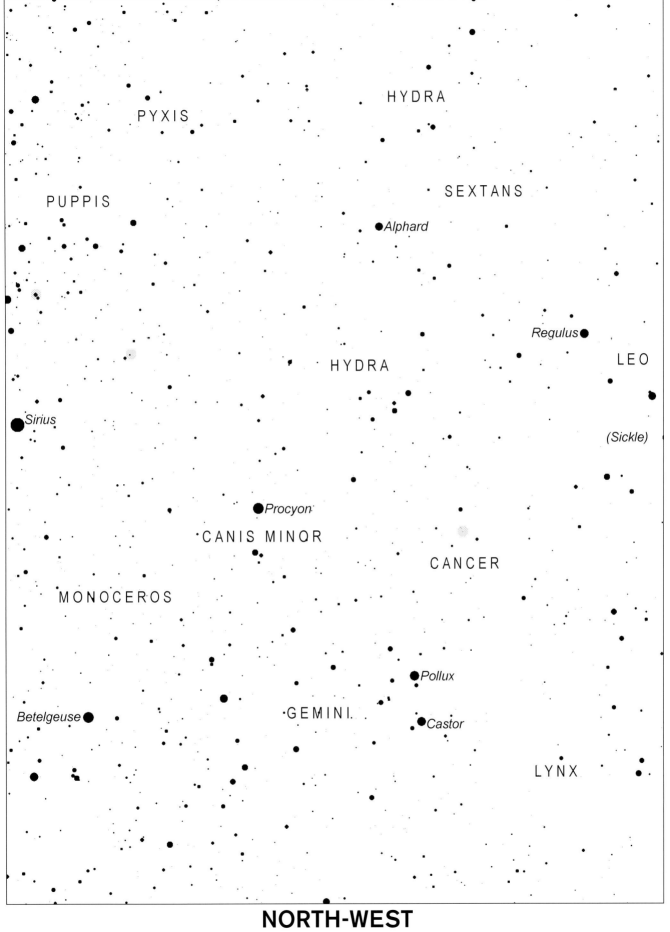

HYDRA

PYXIS

PUPPIS

SEXTANS

●Alphard

Regulus●

LEO

HYDRA

(Sickle)

Sirius

●Procyon

CANIS MINOR

CANCER

MONOCEROS

Pollux●

Betelgeuse●

GEMINI

●Castor

LYNX

NORTH-WEST

JANUARY	FEBRUARY	MARCH	**APRIL**	MAY

04h   03h   02h   01h   00h   23h   22h   **21h**   20h   19h   18h

SET 5
MAY AT 21H

USE ALSO IN JUNE AT 19H, APRIL AT 23H, MARCH AT 01H, FEBRUARY AT 03H

AT OTHER TIMES IN MAY, USE: SET 4 AT 19H, SET 6 AT 23H, SET 7 AT 01H, SET 8 AT 03H, SET 9 AT 05H

HIGHLIGHT OF THE SKY TONIGHT

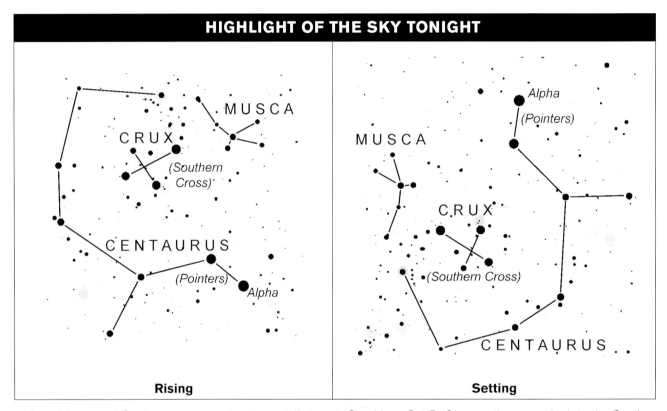

Rising

Setting

Crux, Musca and Centaurus are prominent constellations in Star Maps Set 5. *Observe them very high in the South.*

A guided tour of the sky

Some bright stars in the constellation of Ursa Maior are visible low in the **North**. They are well known in Europe because they form part of the Plough, a group of stars as famous over there as the Southern Cross is in our hemisphere. Coma Berenices is a large cluster visible above the stars of Ursa Maior. This cluster is an interesting subject for binocular-viewing. High up, the Corvus constellation is visible near the sky's summit.

High in the **North-East,** Arcturus glows bright orange. It belongs to the constellation Bootes, which looks like an inverted kite. Diagonally below Bootes is

Corona Borealis (the Northern Crown). Spica, a bright star in Virgo, is high in the sky near Corvus.

The Libra constellation is due **East**. Below Libra are the Ophiuchus and Serpens constellations. To the right of them is Scorpius, an easy constellation to spot because of its impressive size and bright, curved tail. The brightest star in Scorpius, Antares, is strikingly red.

In the **South-East**, the constellation of Sagittarius is visible near the horizon. To the right is Corona Australis, the Southern Crown constellation. Centaurus, with its many bright stars, is high up in the Milky Way. The Pointer stars are the brightest pair of stars in Centaurus.

Apart from our Sun, Alpha (one of the Pointers) is our nearest star. When you look through a telescope, you can see that Alpha Centauri is actually a binary star or set of twins. These twin stars constantly orbit each other, and take eighty years to complete one cycle.

Crux, the Southern Cross, can be seen at its highest position in the sky, due **South**. It is a jewel, ideal for viewing using binoculars. Close by, you can see a black cloud of interstellar dust, enough matter to form hundreds of new stars. The constellation of Carina lies to the right, famous for its wonderful Nebula. In a dark sky the Nebula is easily visible to the naked eye, but binoculars reveal more detail.

You can find the False Cross high in the **South-West**. It appears to mimic the Crux constellation, but the False Cross is much larger. Bright Canopus is lower in the sky. It is a far outlying star in the Carina constellation.

Looking **West** you can see the two Dog constellations, Canis Maior and Canis Minor. Both are near the horizon. If you wait, you can see them setting below the horizon. Sirius in Canis Maior is the brightest star in the sky after our Sun. Alphard is directly above Procyon in Canis Minor. Alphard is the most interesting star in the very long constellation of Hydra (the Water Snake), which stretches across the sky from Procyon to Spica.

Low in the **North-West**, the constellation of Cancer is difficult to identify, but Leo is high up and quite easy to spot. Regulus is bright, acting as the handle of the Sickle. The opposite end of the constellation of Leo is clearly marked by the star Denebola.

The Southern Cross with its dark nebula and open clusters

Star partners

Perhaps as many as one third of all stars are single. Most stars have partners and belong to systems consisting of two or more stars.

Some double stars can be seen using just binoculars, but in order to identify a lot more of them, you should use a telescope. However, only the nearest pairs can be 'split up'.

NEW MOON IN MAY

The week around new Moon is ideal for stargazing. A May new Moon will occur:

Year	Day	Year	Day
2004	19th	2014	28th
2005	8th	2015	18th
2006	27th	2016	6th
2007	16th	2017	25th
2008	5th	2018	15th
2009	24th	2019	5th
2010	14th	2020	22nd
2011	3rd	2021	11th
2012	21st	2022	30th
2013	10th		

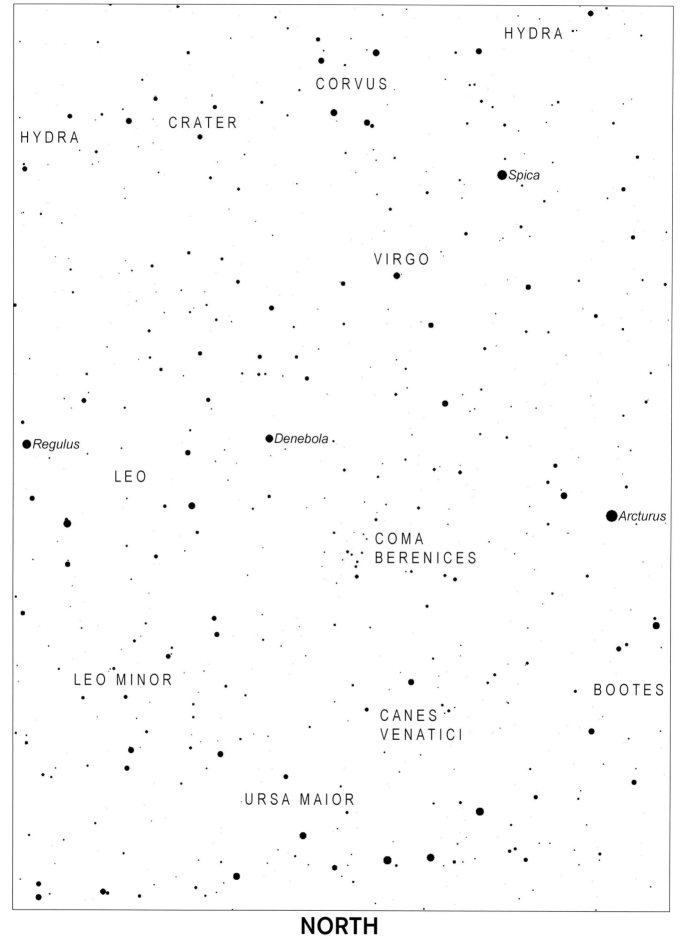

HYDRA

CORVUS

CRATER

HYDRA

●Spica

VIRGO

●Regulus

●Denebola

LEO

●Arcturus

COMA
BERENICES

LEO MINOR

BOOTES

CANES
VENATICI

URSA MAIOR

NORTH

FEBRUARY	MARCH	APRIL	**MAY**	JUNE
04h 03h 02h	01h 00h	23h 22h	**21h** 20h	19h 18h

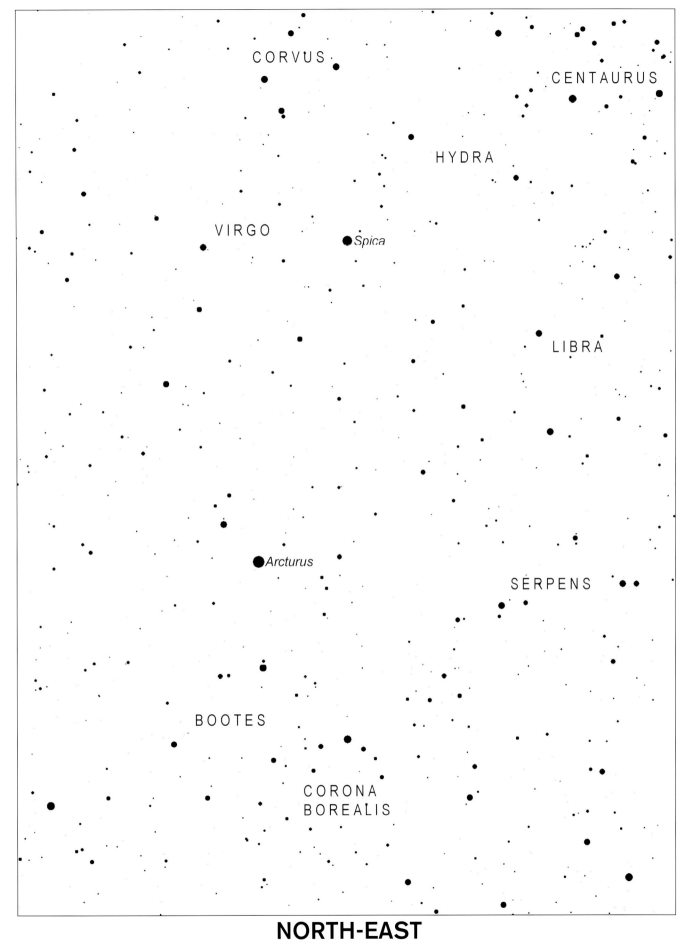

CORVUS

CENTAURUS

HYDRA

VIRGO

●*Spica*

LIBRA

SERPENS

●*Arcturus*

BOOTES

CORONA
BOREALIS

NORTH-EAST

FEBRUARY		MARCH		APRIL		**MAY**		JUNE	
04h	03h	02h	01h	00h	23h	22h	**21h**	20h	19h	18h

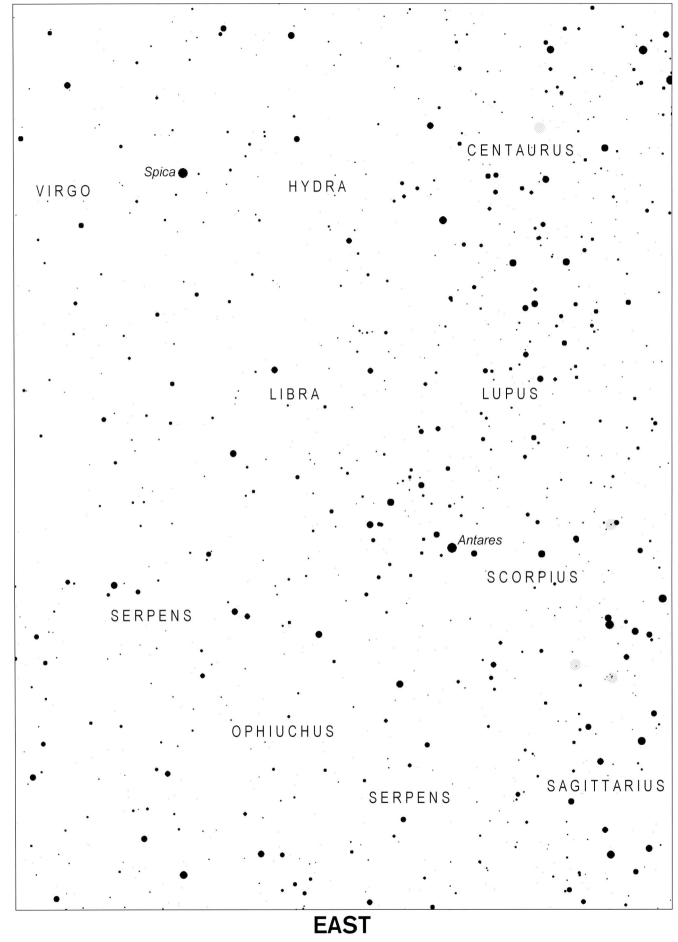

VIRGO

Spica

HYDRA

CENTAURUS

LIBRA

LUPUS

Antares

SCORPIUS

SERPENS

OPHIUCHUS

SERPENS

SAGITTARIUS

EAST

| FEBRUARY | MARCH | APRIL | **MAY** | JUNE |
| 04h 03h | 02h 01h | 00h 23h 22h | **21h** 20h | 19h 18h |

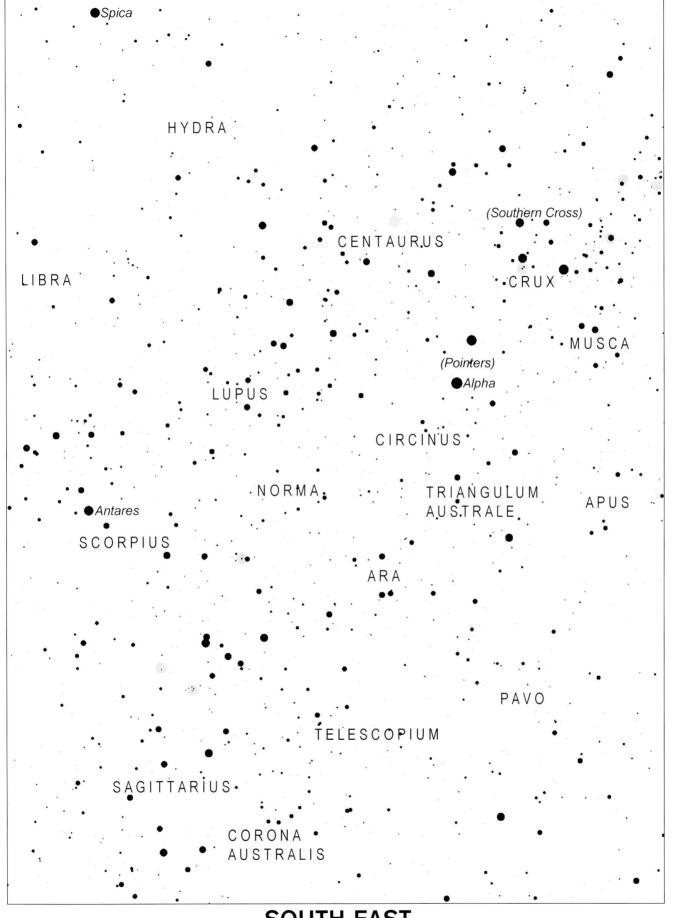

●Spica

HYDRA

(Southern Cross)

CENTAURUS

LIBRA

CRUX

MUSCA

(Pointers)

●Alpha

LUPUS

CIRCINUS

NORMA

TRIANGULUM
AUSTRALE

APUS

●Antares

SCORPIUS

ARA

PAVO

TELESCOPIUM

SAGITTARIUS

CORONA
AUSTRALIS

SOUTH-EAST

	FEBRUARY		MARCH		APRIL		**MAY**		JUNE	
04h	03h	02h	01h	00h	23h	22h	**21h**	20h	19h	18h

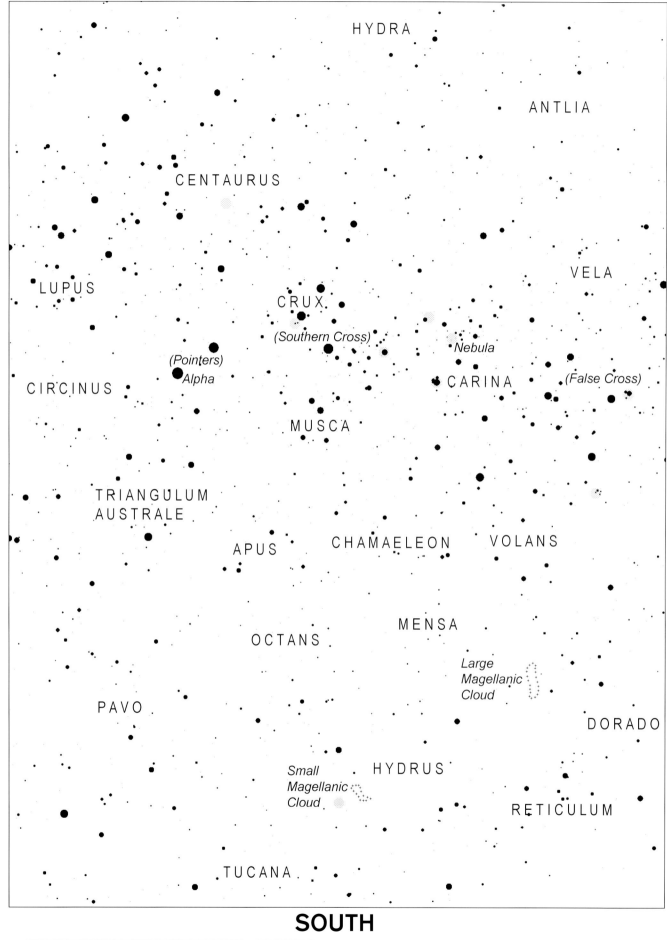

HYDRA

ANTLIA

CENTAURUS

VELA

LUPUS

CRUX

(Southern Cross)

Nebula

(False Cross)

(Pointers)
Alpha

CIRCINUS

CARINA

MUSCA

TRIANGULUM
AUSTRALE

APUS

CHAMAELEON

VOLANS

MENSA

OCTANS

Large
Magellanic
Cloud

PAVO

DORADO

Small
Magellanic
Cloud

HYDRUS

RETICULUM

TUCANA

SOUTH

	FEBRUARY		MARCH		APRIL		**MAY**		JUNE	
04h	03h	02h	01h	00h	23h	22h	**21h**	20h	19h	18h

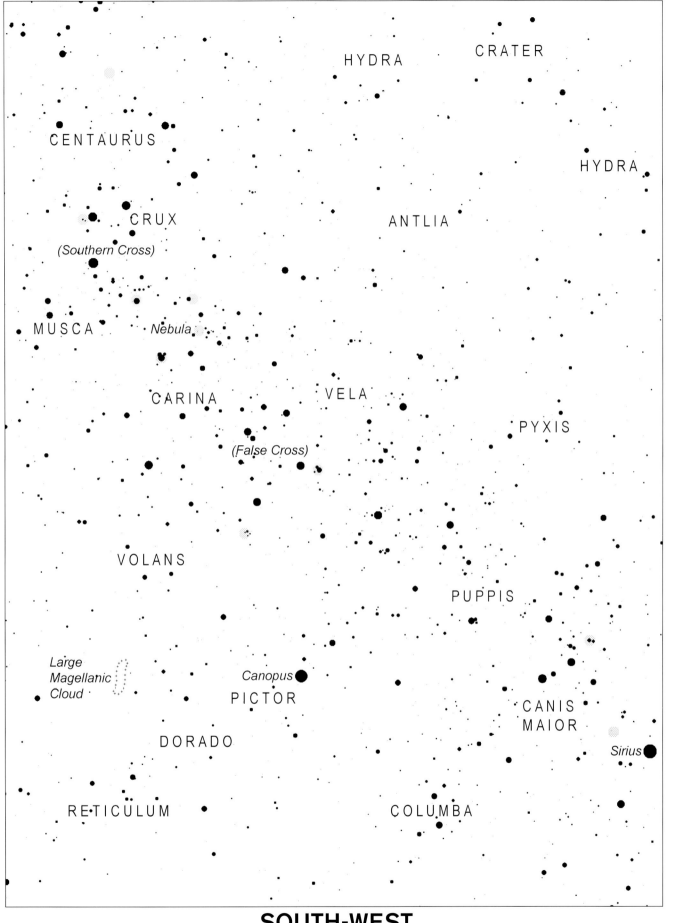

HYDRA

CRATER

CENTAURUS

HYDRA

CRUX

ANTLIA

(Southern Cross)

MUSCA   *Nebula*

CARINA

VELA

PYXIS

(False Cross)

VOLANS

PUPPIS

*Large
Magellanic
Cloud*

Canopus

PICTOR

CANIS
MAIOR

DORADO

Sirius

RETICULUM

COLUMBA

SOUTH-WEST

FEBRUARY		MARCH		APRIL		**MAY**		JUNE	
04h	03h	02h	01h	00h	23h	22h	**21h**	20h	19h	18h

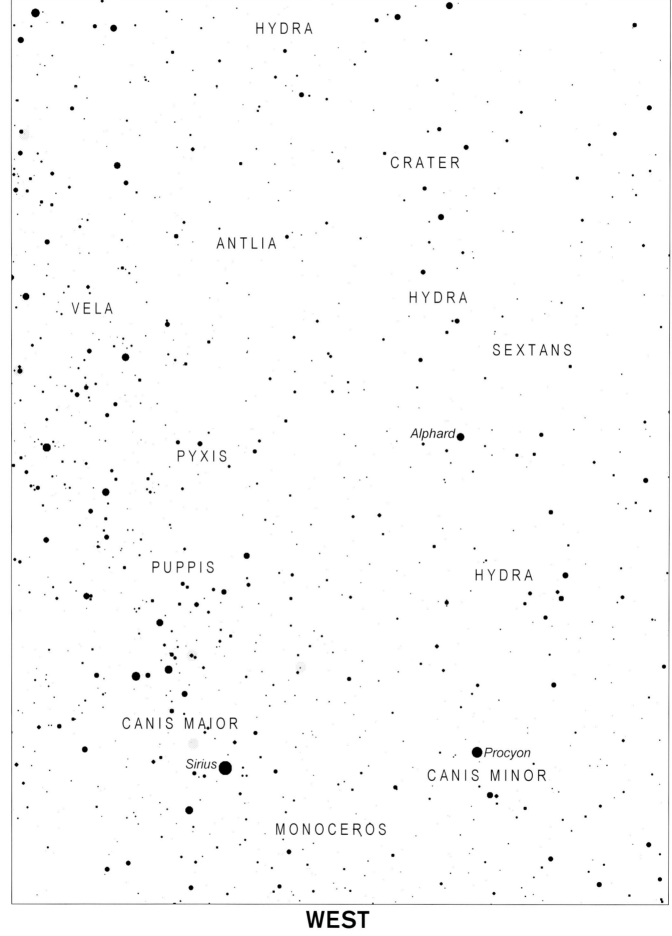

HYDRA

CRATER

ANTLIA

VELA

HYDRA

SEXTANS

PYXIS

Alphard

PUPPIS

HYDRA

CANIS MAJOR

Procyon

Sirius

CANIS MINOR

MONOCEROS

WEST

FEBRUARY	MARCH	APRIL	**MAY**	JUNE
04h 03h	02h 01h	00h 23h	22h **21h**	20h 19h 18h

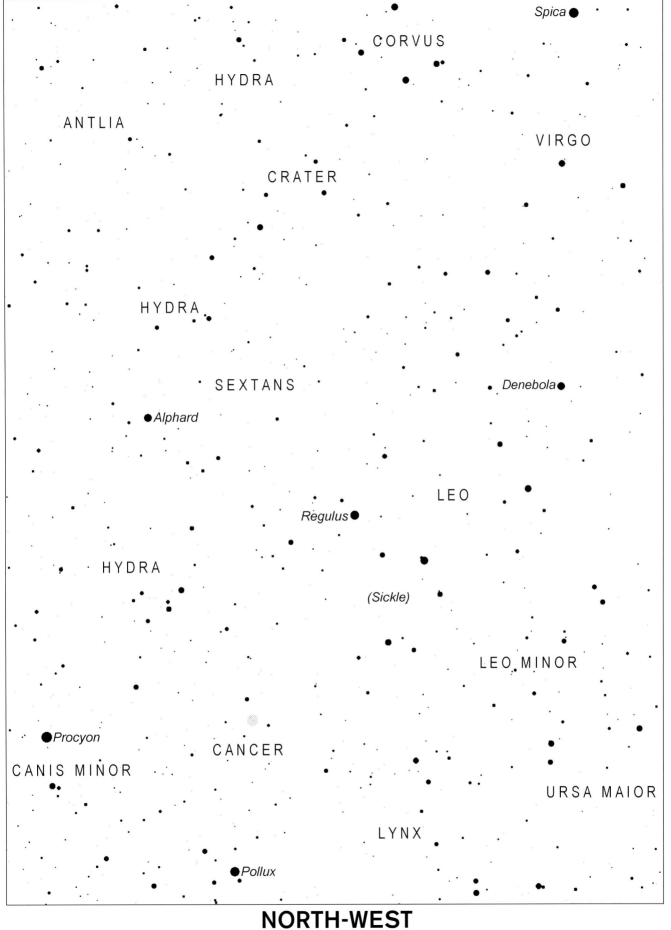

Spica

CORVUS

HYDRA

ANTLIA

VIRGO

CRATER

HYDRA

SEXTANS

Denebola

Alphard

LEO

Regulus

(Sickle)

HYDRA

LEO MINOR

Procyon

CANCER

CANIS MINOR

URSA MAIOR

LYNX

Pollux

NORTH-WEST

	FEBRUARY		MARCH		APRIL		**MAY**		JUNE	
04h	03h	02h	01h	00h	23h	22h	**21h**	20h	19h	18h

SET 6
JUNE AT 21H
USE ALSO IN JULY AT 19H, MAY AT 23H, APRIL AT 01H, MARCH 03H

AT OTHER TIMES IN **JUNE**, USE: **SET 5** AT 19H, **SET 7** AT 23H, **SET 8** AT 01H, **SET 9** AT 03H, **SET 10** AT 05H

HIGHLIGHT OF THE SKY TONIGHT

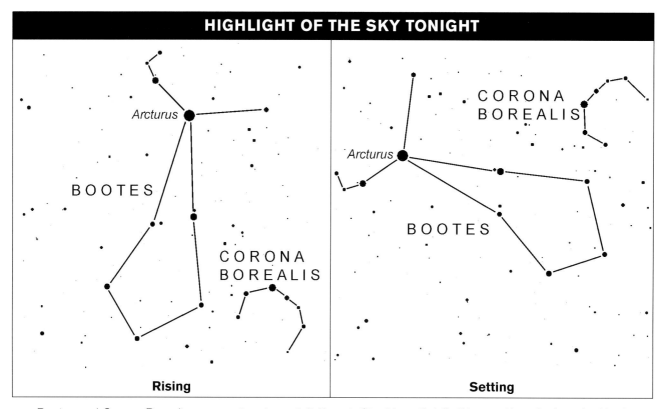

Rising

Setting

Bootes and Corona Borealis are prominent constellations in Star Maps Set 6. *Observe them high in the North.*

A guided tour of the sky

The bright orange glow of Arcturus is striking, due **North**. It forms part of the Bootes constellation. To the left, near the horizon, are some stars of the constellation Ursa Maior. To the right, the finely shaped constellation of Corona Borealis (the Northern Crown) can be seen.

Libra's constellation is high in the **North-East**. It is difficult to identify, as are the constellations of Serpens and Ophiuchus, which are large but lack bright stars. Hercules may prove even more difficult to spot, low in the sky.

Scorpius stands out prominently in the **East**. Its brightest star, Antares, is strikingly red. Lower in the sky

is the Sagittarius constellation, where the Milky Way is at its brightest. Use binoculars to examine the detail in this part of our galaxy.

To the right of Sagittarius, in the **South-East**, Corona Australis (the Southern Crown constellation) is visible. It looks glorious through ordinary binoculars. The apparent close arrangement of these stars is an illusion – they are at hugely different distances from Earth and do not form a cluster. High up in the Norma constellation, the dark lane in the Milky Way divides into two branches. This lane and its branches are produced by clouds of interstellar dust that impede our view of distant

Omega Centauri is a spectacular globular cluster

the sky's summit. Its brightest star is Alphard, close to the horizon. Much higher up, Corvus shines brightly in an apparently empty expanse of sky.

Bright Spica shines high in the **North-West** and forms part of the constellation of Virgo. Far below is Leo. Look for the Sickle by identifying bright Regulus as its handle. Denebola marks the opposite end of Leo. To the right of Denebola you can see Coma Berenices, if the sky is dark enough. This cluster is difficult to see with the naked eye but is ideal for binocular observation.

The beginning of a star

Stars are created in the centres of nebulae. The term 'nebula' is Latin for haze, and refers to a huge cloud of gas and dust in space. When gravity causes such a cloud to contract, hundreds or even thousands of new stars are produced – the birth of a new cluster.

Bright nebulae become visible either because new stars illuminate the dust or when they cause the gas to glow dimly. Both light-producing processes may occur in one nebula.

However, if bright young stars are absent, nebulae can show up only as dark silhouettes against a starry background.

stars. This dust is the material from which many new stars will be formed in the distant future.

The two Pointer stars, due **South**, are at their highest position. They help us to find Crux (the Southern Cross). The Pointers are the brightest stars in the constellation of Centaurus. Most of its stars are higher up, together with those of the Lupus constellation. One of the Pointers, Alpha Centauri, is a binary star or set of twins, which may be seen with a telescope.

To the right, towards the **South-West**, Crux, the Southern Cross constellation, can be seen. Not far below it is the striking Nebula in the constellation of Carina. Both Crux and Carina's Nebula look wonderful through binoculars. Still lower is the False Cross and lower still is the bright star Canopus.

In the **West**, the extended constellation of Hydra (the Water Snake) is visible, stretching from the horizon to

NEW MOON IN JUNE			
The week around new Moon is ideal for stargazing. A June new Moon will occur:			
Year	Day	Year	Day
2004	17th	2014	27th
2005	6th	2015	16th
2006	25th	2016	5th
2007	15th	2017	24th
2008	3rd	2018	13th
2009	22nd	2019	3rd
2010	12th	2020	21st
2011	1st	2021	10th
2012	19th	2022	29th
2013	8th		

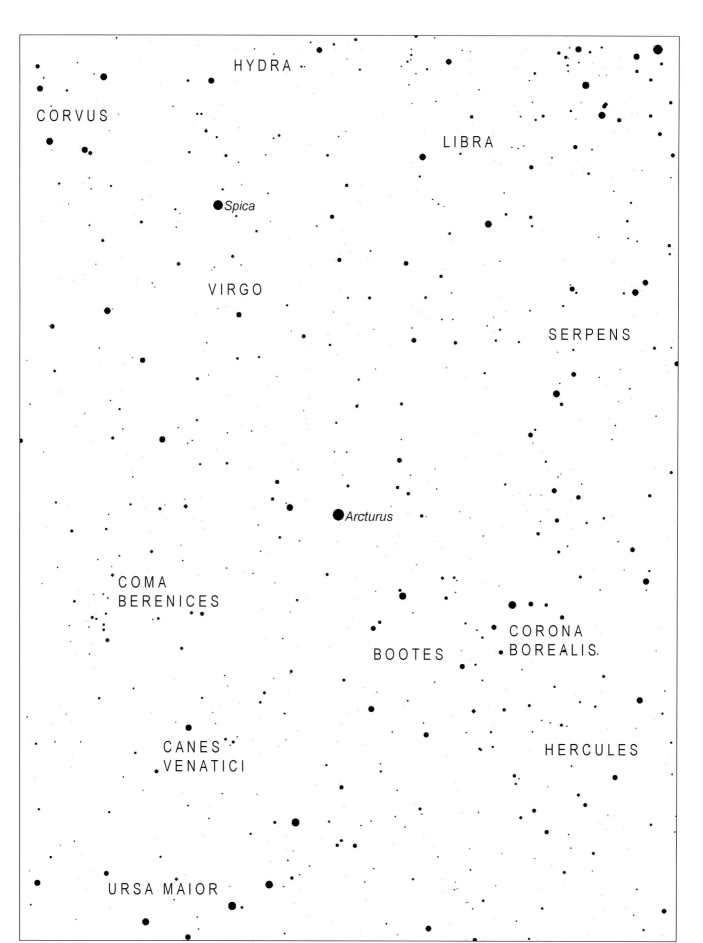

HYDRA

CORVUS

LIBRA

●Spica

VIRGO

SERPENS

●Arcturus

COMA
BERENICES

BOOTES

CORONA
BOREALIS.

CANES
VENATICI

HERCULES

URSA MAIOR

NORTH

	MARCH		APRIL		MAY		**JUNE**		JULY	
04h	03h	02h	01h	00h	23h	22h	**21h**	20h	19h	18h

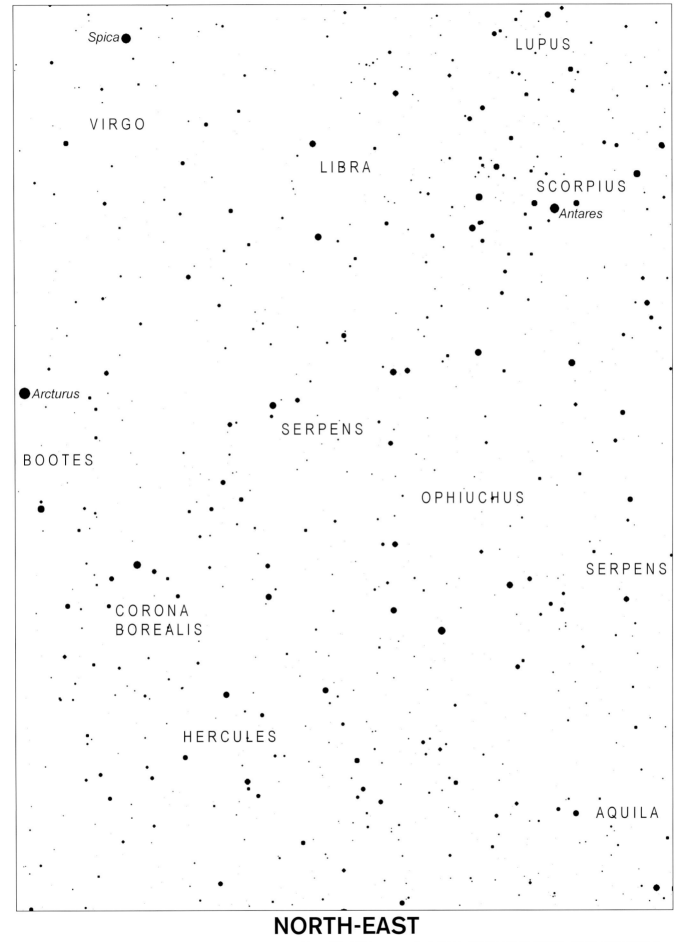

Spica

LUPUS

VIRGO

LIBRA

SCORPIUS

Antares

Arcturus

SERPENS

BOOTES

OPHIUCHUS

SERPENS

CORONA
BOREALIS

HERCULES

AQUILA

NORTH-EAST

MARCH	APRIL	MAY	JUNE	JULY
04h 03h 02h	01h 00h	23h 22h	**21h** 20h	19h 18h

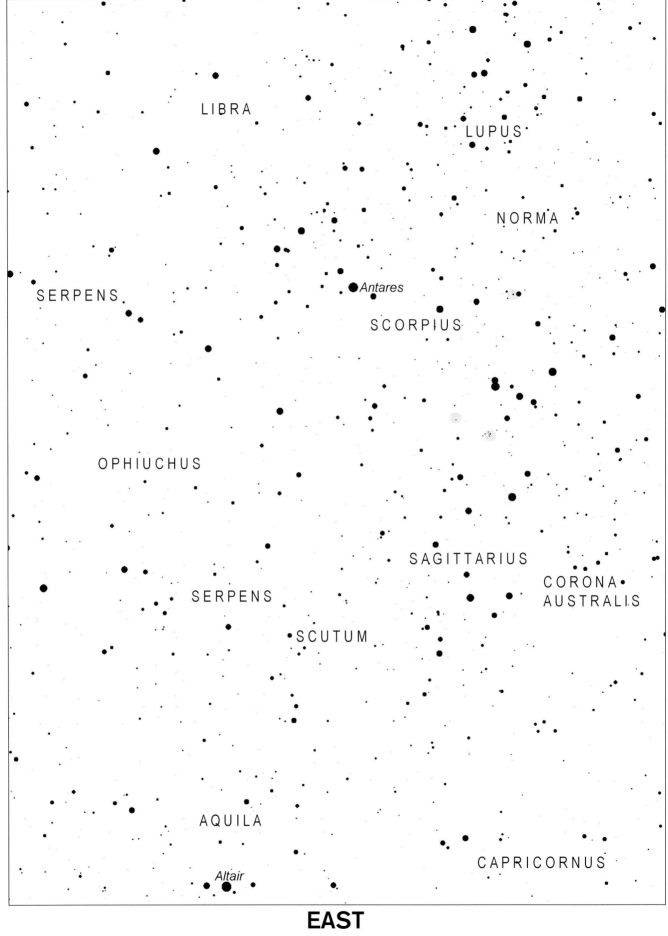

LIBRA

LUPUS

NORMA

SERPENS

● *Antares*

SCORPIUS

OPHIUCHUS

SAGITTARIUS

SERPENS

CORONA
AUSTRALIS

SCUTUM

AQUILA

CAPRICORNUS

Altair

EAST

MARCH	APRIL	MAY	**JUNE**	JULY
04h 03h 02h	01h 00h	23h 22h	**21h** 20h	19h 18h

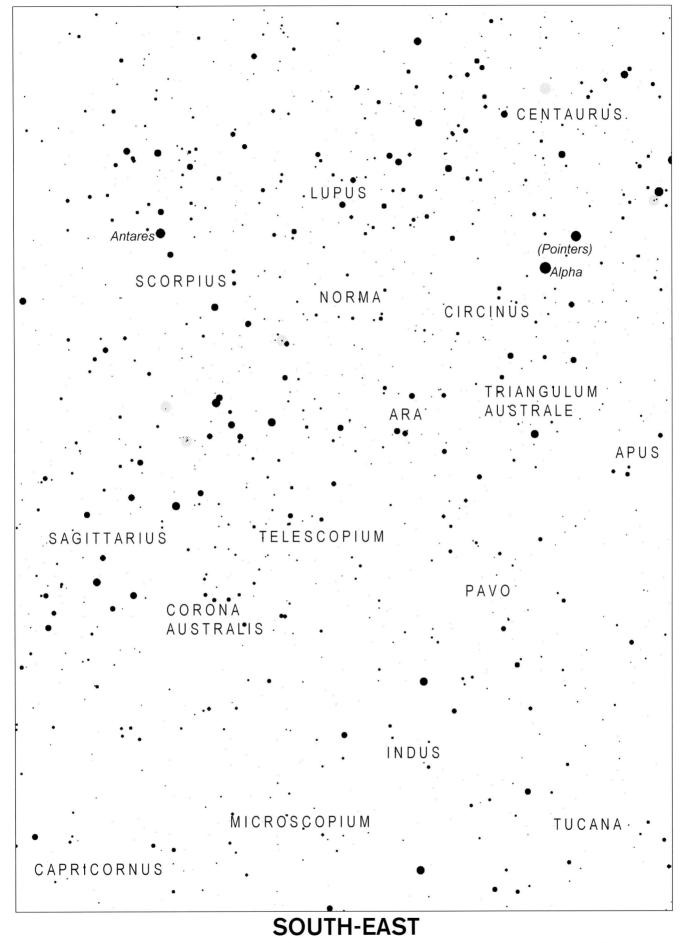

CENTAURUS

LUPUS

Antares

SCORPIUS

NORMA

(Pointers)
Alpha

CIRCINUS

TRIANGULUM
AUSTRALE

ARA

APUS

SAGITTARIUS

TELESCOPIUM

PAVO

CORONA
AUSTRALIS

INDUS

MICROSCOPIUM

TUCANA

CAPRICORNUS

SOUTH-EAST

	MARCH	APRIL	MAY	**JUNE**	JULY	
04h	03h	02h	01h	00h	23h	22h	**21h**	20h	19h	18h

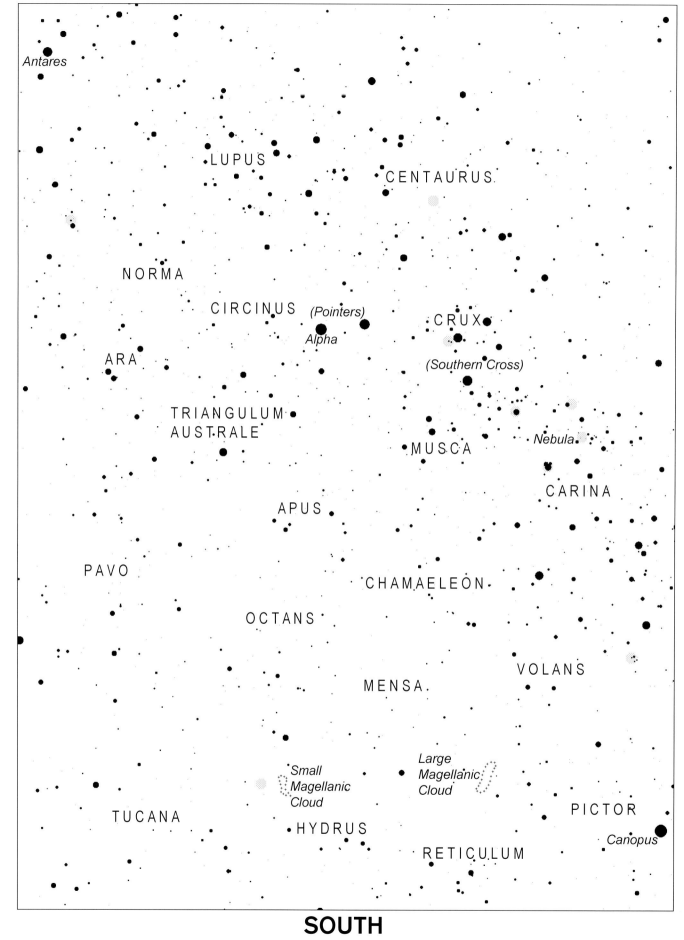

Antares

LUPUS

CENTAURUS

NORMA

CIRCINUS (Pointers)

Alpha

CRUX

ARA

(Southern Cross)

TRIANGULUM
AUSTRALE

MUSCA

Nebula

CARINA

APUS

PAVO

CHAMAELEON

OCTANS

VOLANS

MENSA

Small
Magellanic
Cloud

Large
Magellanic
Cloud

TUCANA

PICTOR

Canopus

HYDRUS

RETICULUM

SOUTH

| | MARCH | | APRIL | | MAY | | JUNE | | JULY | |
| 04h | 03h | 02h | 01h | 00h | 23h | 22h | 21h | 20h | 19h | 18h |

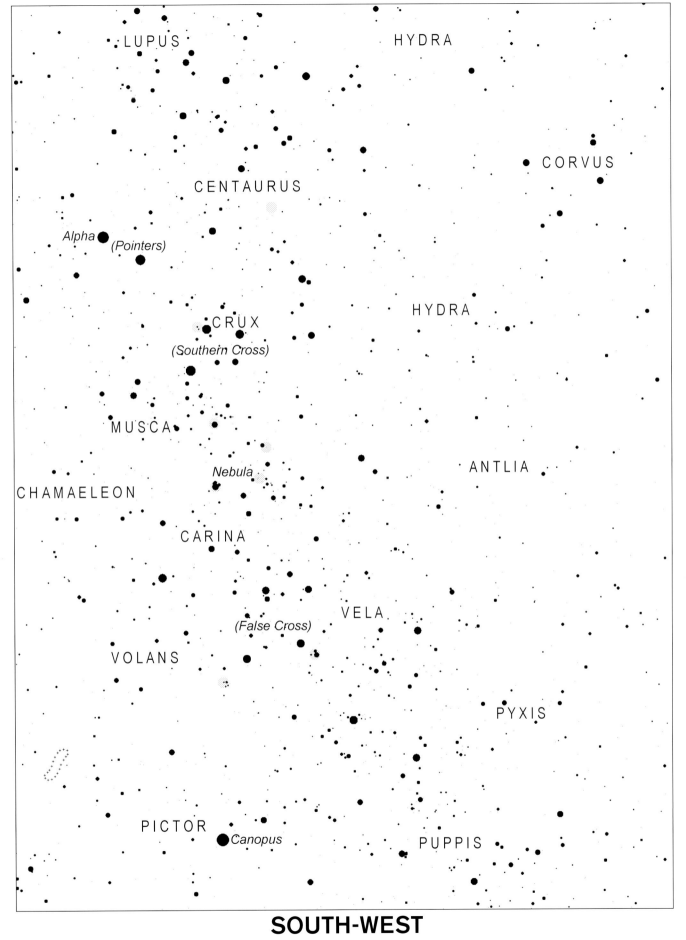

LUPUS

HYDRA

CORVUS

CENTAURUS

Alpha
(Pointers)

HYDRA

CRUX
(Southern Cross)

MUSCA

ANTLIA

CHAMAELEON

Nebula

CARINA

VELA

(False Cross)

VOLANS

PYXIS

PICTOR
Canopus

PUPPIS

SOUTH-WEST

	MARCH		APRIL		MAY		**JUNE**		JULY	
04h	03h	02h	01h	00h	23h	22h	**21h**	20h	19h	18h

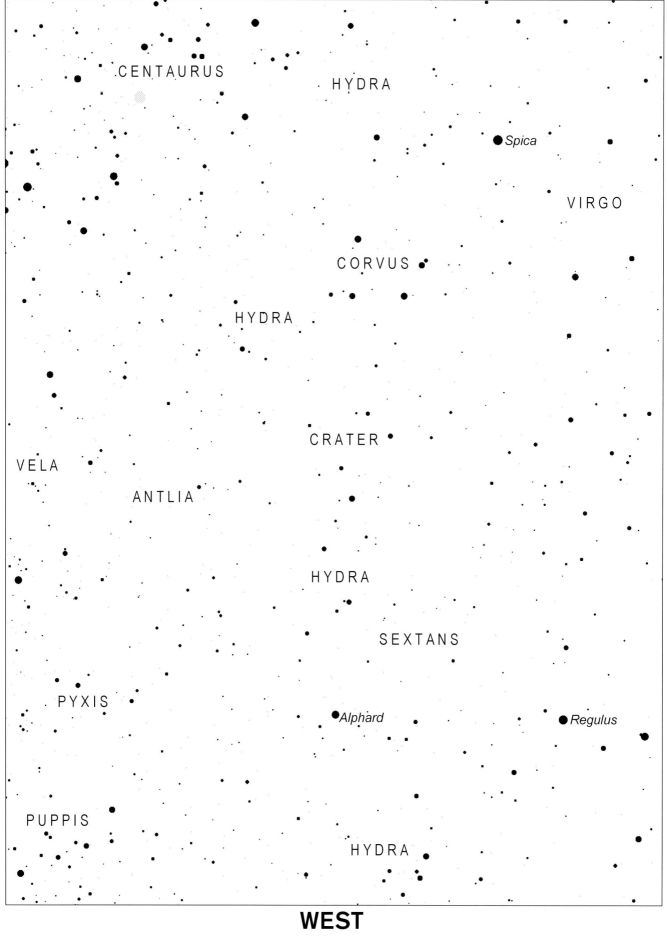

CENTAURUS

HYDRA

● *Spica*

VIRGO

CORVUS

HYDRA

CRATER

VELA

ANTLIA

HYDRA

SEXTANS

PYXIS

●*Alphard*

●*Regulus*

PUPPIS

HYDRA

WEST

	MARCH		APRIL		MAY		**JUNE**		JULY	
04h	03h	02h	01h	00h	23h	22h	**21h**	20h	19h	18h

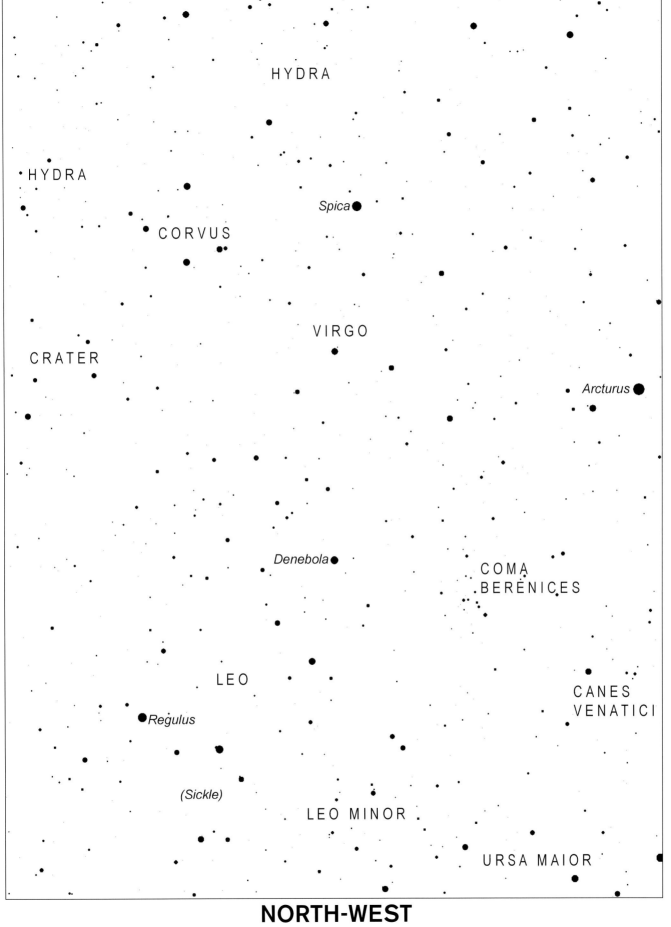

HYDRA

HYDRA

CORVUS

Spica

CRATER

VIRGO

Arcturus

Denebola

COMA
BERENICES

LEO

CANES
VENATICI

Regulus

(Sickle)

LEO MINOR

URSA MAIOR

NORTH-WEST

	MARCH		APRIL		MAY		**JUNE**		JULY	
04h	03h	02h	01h	00h	23h	22h	**21h**	20h	19h	18h

SET 7
JULY AT 21H
USE ALSO IN JUNE 23H, MAY AT 01H, APRIL AT 03H, MARCH AT 05H

AT OTHER TIMES IN JULY, USE: SET 6 AT 19H, SET 8 AT 23H, SET 9 AT 01H, SET 10 AT 03H, SET 11 AT 05H

HIGHLIGHT OF THE SKY TONIGHT

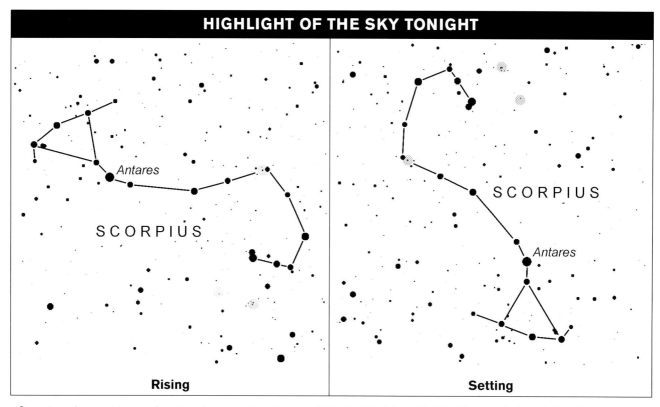

Rising

Setting

Scorpius, shown rising and setting, is a prominent constellation in Star Maps Set 7. *Observe it almost directly above you.*

A guided tour of the sky

The giant constellation of Scorpius lies almost overhead. Red Antares is its brightest star.

Looking **North**, you can see Corona Borealis (the Northern Crown constellation). The Hercules constellation is visible to its right. Higher up is one part of Serpens with huge Ophiuchus further right. All three constellations are hard to identify because they lack bright stars and are spread over a large expanse of sky.

Bright stars are rising in the **North-East**. To the left is the star Vega, part of the Lyra constellation. The dim star just below Vega shows up as a binary or twin star through binoculars. To the right is bright Altair in the constellation Aquila. Altair is quite easy to identify by its 'companions'. Higher in the sky is the other part of the Serpens constellation, near a bright Milky Way cloud in the dim, inconspicuous constellation of Scutum.

In the **East** you can see the Capricornus constellation, shaped like a distorted triangle. High up is beautiful Sagittarius, where the Milky Way is brightest. Using binoculars, if possible, look for Corona Australis (the Southern Crown constellation). The stars in Corona Australis are at greatly different distances from Earth and their apparent arrangement is purely accidental.

Comet Hyakutake with bright star Arcturus

The star in the **West** shines brightly. It is Spica and is part of the Virgo constellation. Libra is far above Virgo. Left of Spica, and lower down, the Corvus constellation is visible. The stars in Corvus are not bright, but can easily be seen when the sky is dark enough.

Looking **North-West**, the bright orange star is Arcturus. It belongs to the kite-shaped constellation Bootes. The star on the left is Denebola, near the horizon.

New generations

Dying stars send a large proportion of their mass back into space. There is no reason why this material could not aggregate into nebulae, hence creating new generations of stars. This process appears to be a cosmic form of recycling, but it is more than that.

Stars of a new generation are different from the old, because they are made of matter that was processed within older stars. To produce energy, stars must convert light-weight elements, hydrogen and helium, into heavier elements such as carbon, nitrogen, oxygen, silicon, calcium and iron. Therefore, later generations of stars are progressively enriched with heavier and more diverse elements.

Grus is easy to identify – its shape is distinctive. You can see it rather low in the **South-East**. Bright Fomalhaut, the only prominent star in the constellation of Piscis Austrinus, shines close to the horizon.

Due **South**, the Norma constellation is visible in a bright part of the Milky Way, where its dark lane divides into two branches. Lower down, two constellations, Ara and Triangulum Australe, can be seen. Achernar is the bright star near the horizon, visible in a clear, dark sky.

The Pointers, the brightest pair of stars in the constellation of Centaurus, are towards the **South-West**. One of the Pointers, Alpha, is the nearest star to our Sun. Just below Alpha is Crux, the Southern Cross constellation. To the left of Crux is a dark spot in the Milky Way – a cloud of interstellar dust that absorbs the light of many stars beyond it. Lower in the sky, the Nebula in Carina is visible, in which new stars are being formed from gas and dust. Below Carina, the so-called False Cross can be seen very near the horizon. However, it will not be visible for long and will soon set.

NEW MOON IN JULY			
The week around new Moon is ideal for stargazing. A July new Moon will occur:			
Year	**Day**	**Year**	**Day**
2004	17th	2014	27th
2005	6th	2015	16th
2006	25th	2016	4th
2007	14th	2017	23rd
2008	3rd	2018	13th
2009	22nd	2019	2nd
2010	11th	2020	20th
2011	1st & 30th	2021	10th
2012	19th	2022	28th
2013	8th		

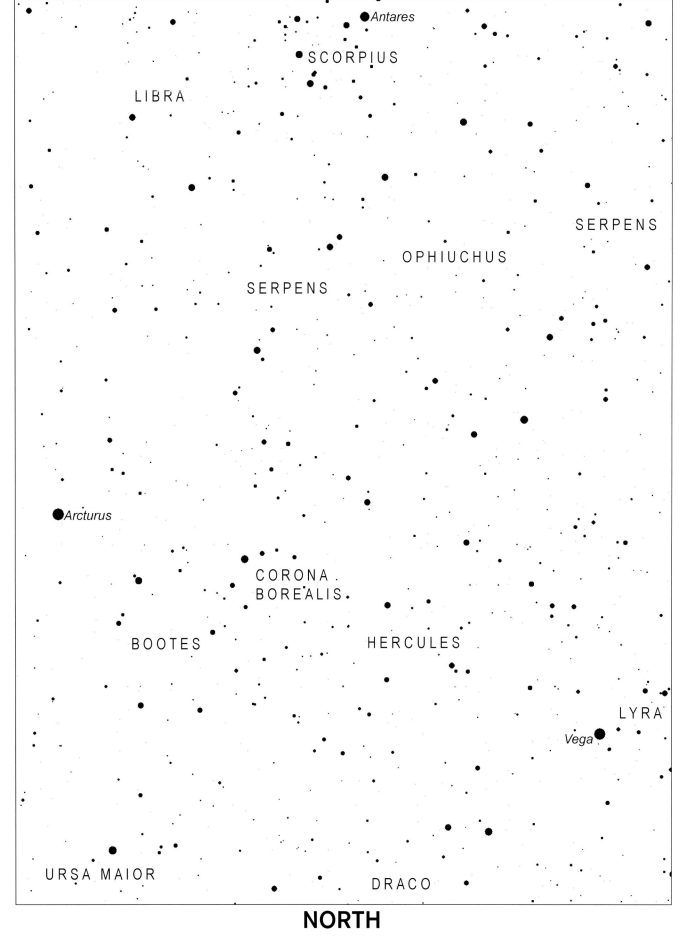

Antares

SCORPIUS

LIBRA

SERPENS

OPHIUCHUS

SERPENS

Arcturus

CORONA
BOREALIS

BOOTES

HERCULES

LYRA

Vega

URSA MAIOR

DRACO

NORTH

MARCH		APRIL		MAY		JUNE		JULY	
06h	05h	04h	03h	02h	01h	00h	23h	22h	**21h**	20h

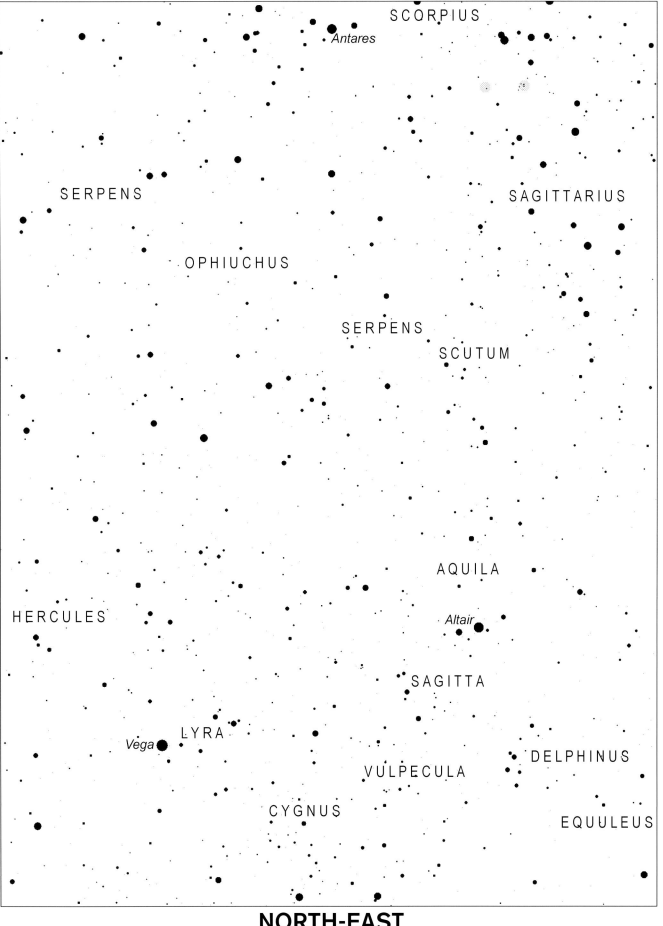

SCORPIUS

Antares

SERPENS

SAGITTARIUS

OPHIUCHUS

SERPENS

SCUTUM

AQUILA

HERCULES

Altair

SAGITTA

LYRA

Vega

DELPHINUS

VULPECULA

CYGNUS

EQUULEUS

NORTH-EAST

| MARCH | | APRIL | | MAY | | JUNE | | **JULY** | |
| 06h | 05h | 04h | 03h | 02h | 01h | 00h | 23h | 22h | **21h** | 20h |

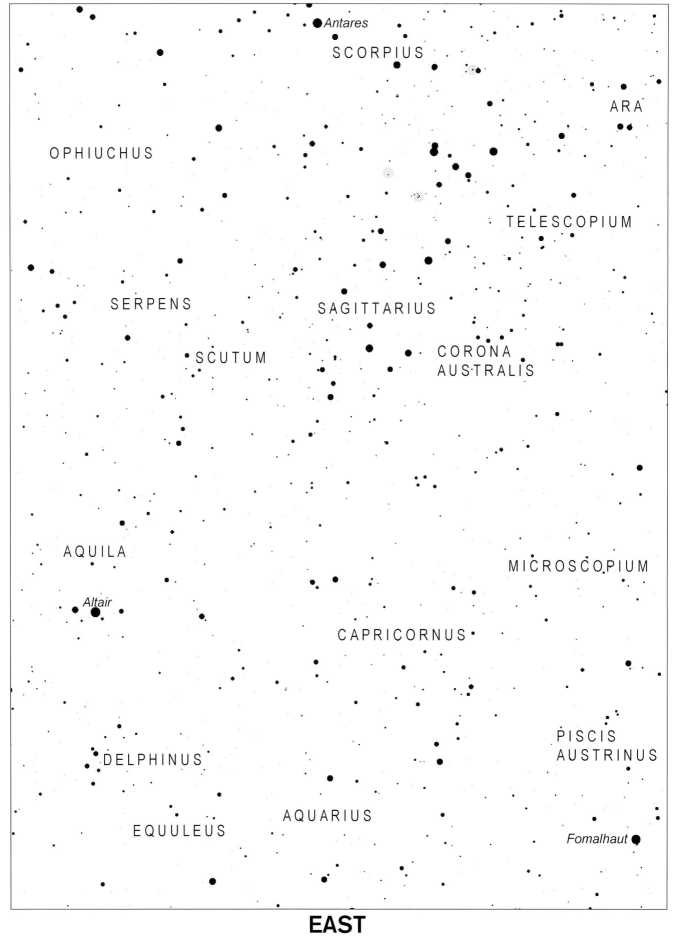

Antares

SCORPIUS

ARA

OPHIUCHUS

TELESCOPIUM

SERPENS

SAGITTARIUS

SCUTUM

CORONA
AUSTRALIS

AQUILA

MICROSCOPIUM

Altair

CAPRICORNUS

PISCIS
AUSTRINUS

DELPHINUS

AQUARIUS

EQUULEUS

Fomalhaut

EAST

	MARCH		APRIL		MAY		JUNE		**JULY**	
06h	05h	04h	03h	02h	01h	00h	23h	22h	**21h**	20h

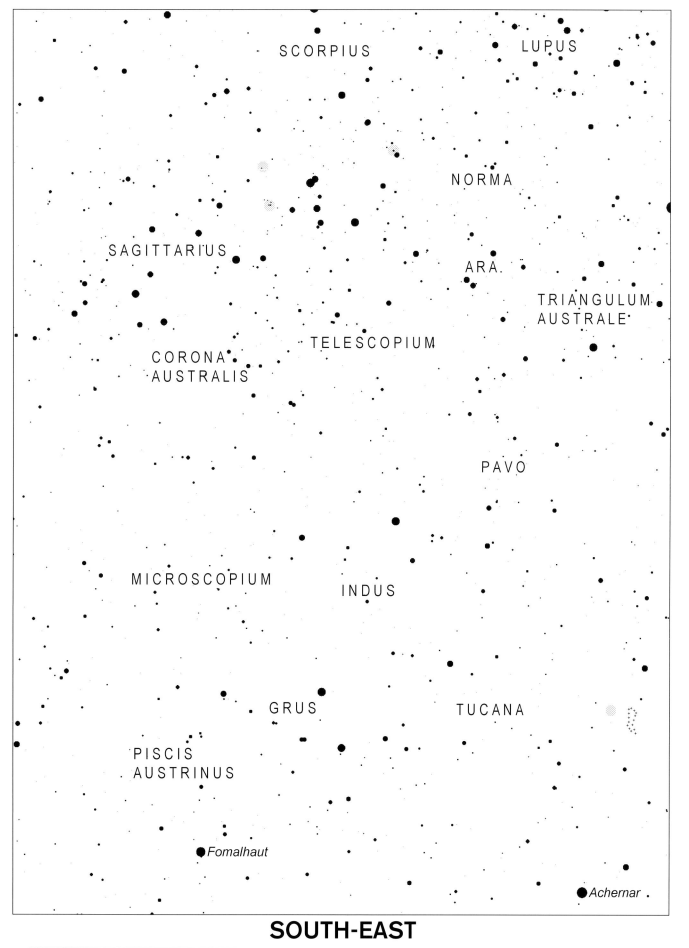

SCORPIUS

LUPUS

NORMA

SAGITTARIUS

ARA

TRIANGULUM
AUSTRALE

TELESCOPIUM

CORONA
AUSTRALIS

PAVO

MICROSCOPIUM

INDUS

GRUS

TUCANA

PISCIS
AUSTRINUS

Fomalhaut

Achernar

SOUTH-EAST

| 06h | MARCH 05h | 04h | APRIL 03h | 02h | MAY 01h | 00h | JUNE 23h | 22h | **JULY 21h** | 20h |

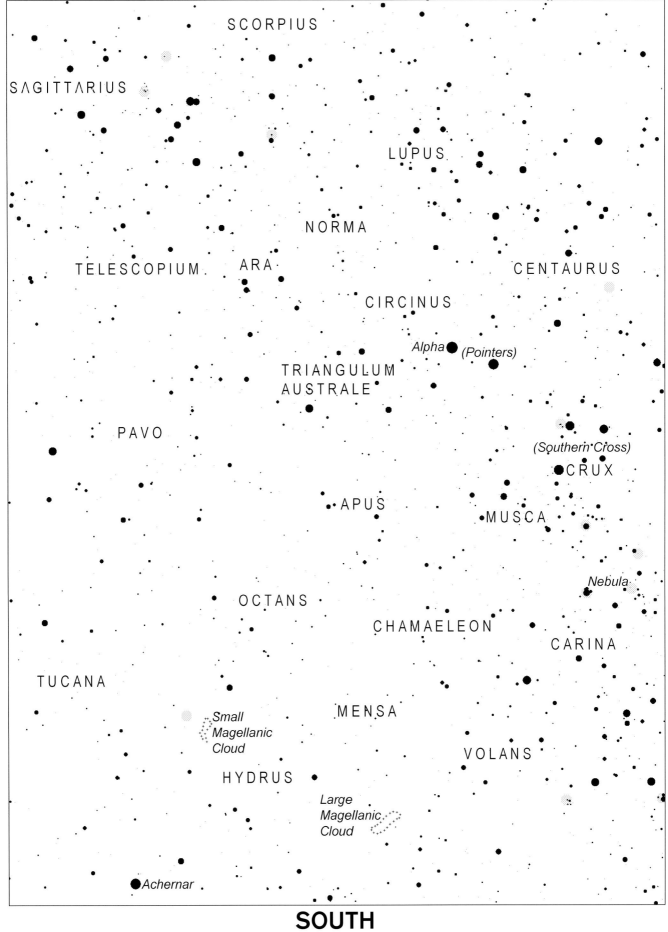

SCORPIUS

SAGITTARIUS

LUPUS

NORMA

TELESCOPIUM   ARA

CENTAURUS

CIRCINUS

Alpha ● (Pointers)

TRIANGULUM
AUSTRALE

(Southern Cross)

PAVO

● CRUX

APUS

MUSCA

Nebula

OCTANS

CHAMAELEON

CARINA

TUCANA

MENSA

Small
Magellanic
Cloud

VOLANS

HYDRUS

Large
Magellanic
Cloud

● Achernar

SOUTH

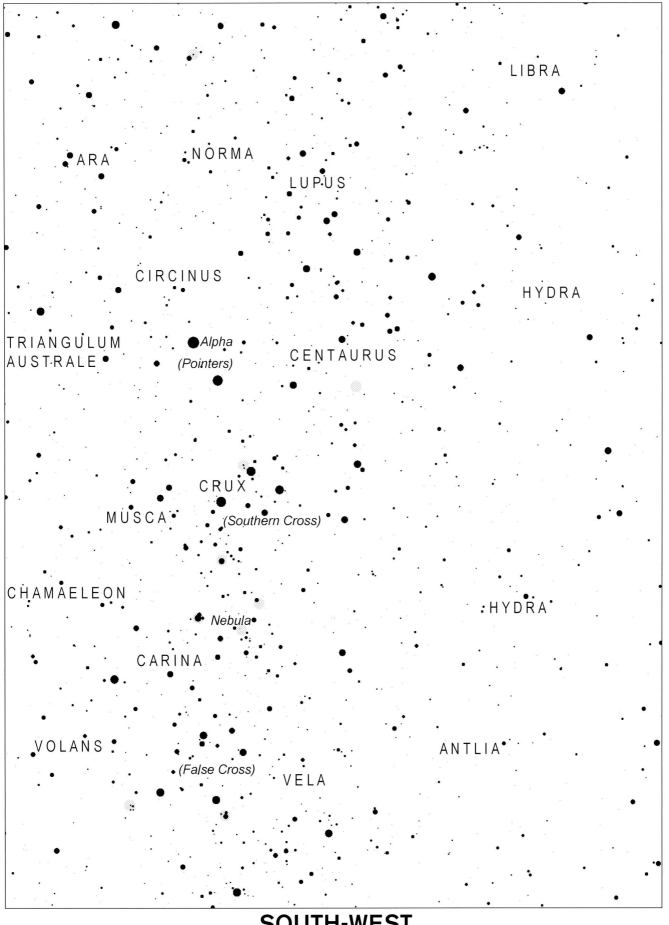

LIBRA

ARA

NORMA

LUPUS

CIRCINUS

HYDRA

TRIANGULUM
AUSTRALE

Alpha
(Pointers)

CENTAURUS

CRUX

MUSCA

(Southern Cross)

CHAMAELEON

HYDRA

Nebula

CARINA

VOLANS

ANTLIA

(False Cross)

VELA

SOUTH-WEST

	MARCH		APRIL		MAY		JUNE		**JULY**	
06h	05h	04h	03h	02h	01h	00h	23h	22h	**21h**	20h

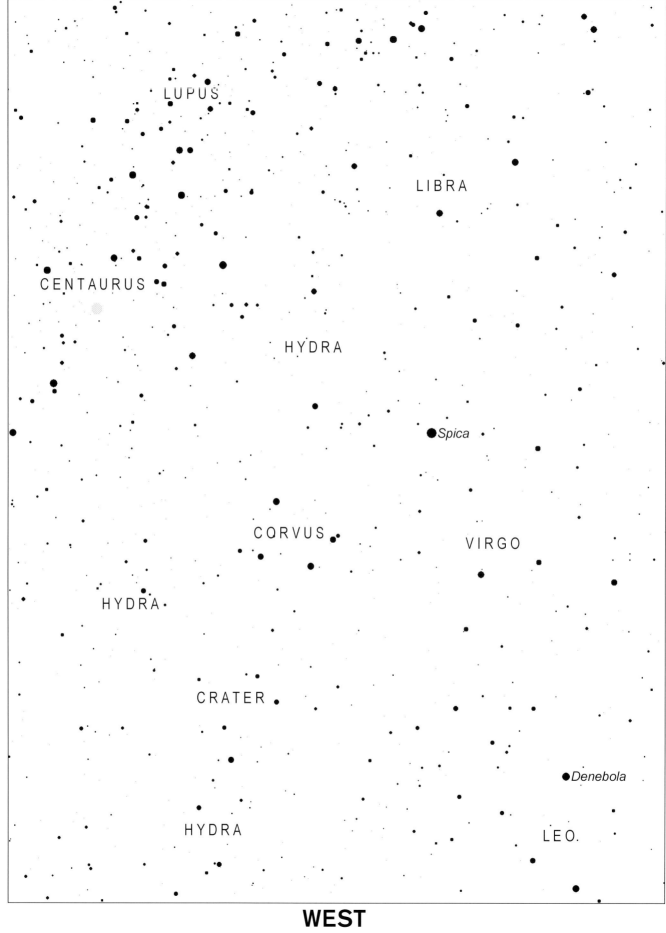

LUPUS

LIBRA

CENTAURUS

HYDRA

Spica

CORVUS

VIRGO

HYDRA

CRATER

Denebola

HYDRA

LEO

WEST

| | MARCH | | APRIL | | MAY | | JUNE | | **JULY** | |
| 06h | 05h | 04h | 03h | 02h | 01h | 00h | 23h | 22h | **21h** | 20h |

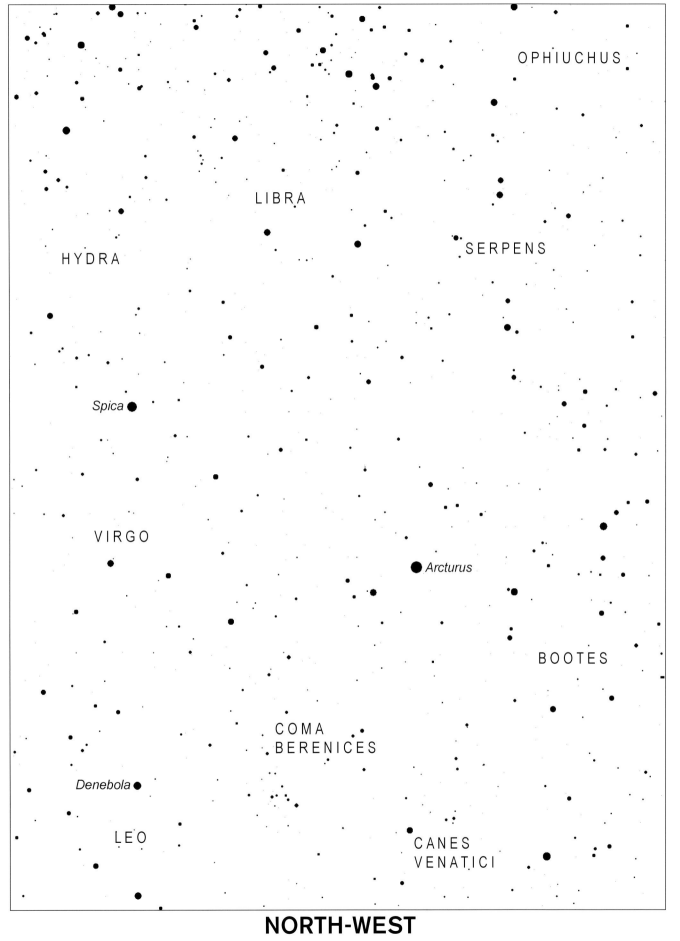

OPHIUCHUS

LIBRA

SERPENS

HYDRA

Spica ●

VIRGO

● *Arcturus*

BOOTES

COMA
BERENICES

Denebola ●

LEO

CANES
VENATICI

NORTH-WEST

	MARCH		APRIL		MAY		JUNE		**JULY**	
06h	05h	04h	03h	02h	01h	00h	23h	22h	**21h**	20h

SET 8
AUGUST AT 21H

USE ALSO IN JULY AT 23H, JUNE AT 01H, MAY AT 03H, APRIL AT 05H

AT OTHER TIMES IN **AUGUST**, USE: **SET 9** AT 23H, **SET 10** AT 01H, **SET 11** AT 03H, AND **SET 12** AT 05H

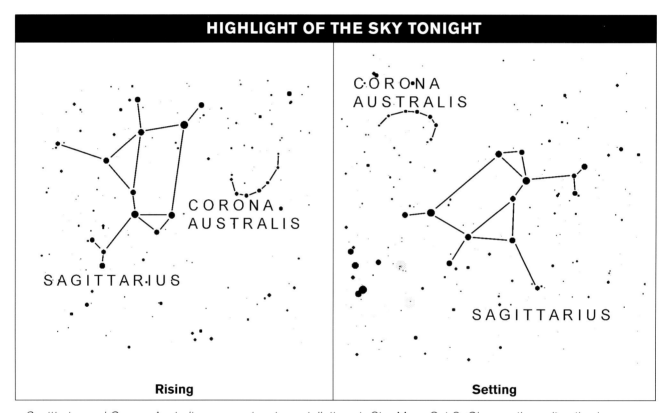

HIGHLIGHT OF THE SKY TONIGHT

Rising   **Setting**

Sagittarius and Corona Australis are prominent constellations in Star Maps Set 8. *Observe them directly above you.*

A guided tour of the sky

Directly overhead is the brightest part of the Milky Way in the constellation of Sagittarius. At this moment, our own Milky Way Galaxy shows itself at its very best.

Rather low in the **North** is the bright star Vega, part of the constellation of Lyra. The faint star slightly below and to the right of Vega is an interesting binary or twin star. The twins are easily seen through binoculars, but a telescope is needed to show that these stars are *four* stars or *two* pairs of twins. The Cygnus constellation, sometimes referred to in the past as the Northern Cross, lies to the right of Lyra, and Deneb is its brightest star.

Much higher in the sky is the star Altair in the constellation Aquila. Deneb, Vega and Altair constitute the so-called Winter Triangle. Tiny Sagitta (the Arrow) is visible below Altair.

Lower than Altair, and due **North-East**, is dim Delphinus (the Dolphin constellation). A dark sky will help you to see it. A few stars are scattered low in the sky, and form part of the constellation of Pegasus.

High up in the **East** you can see Capricornus, a distorted triangle. To its left and further down are the dim stars of the constellation of Aquarius. Further right, Fomalhaut shines conspicuously in Piscis Austrinus.

The Rosette Nebula

The constellation of Grus is visible towards the **South-East**, close to Fomalhaut. High above Grus, Corona Australis (the Southern Crown constellation) can be seen. It is worth examining through binoculars. Far below Grus is the constellation of Phoenix, with the bright star Achernar on the right.

Higher in the sky, and visible to the naked eye in the **South**, is the Small Magellanic Cloud – one of our galaxy's nearest neighbours. Its faint shine has travelled roughly two thousand centuries to reach our eyes. Far above the Small Cloud is the Pavo constellation. Triangulum Australe lies to the right of Pavo, with Ara above it.

Further right and towards the **South-West**, you can identify the two Pointer stars. They are the brightest stars in the constellation of Centaurus. One of the Pointers, Alpha, is the Sun's nearest neighbour. Below the Pointers is Crux, the Southern Cross, and just to its left is a dark spot in the Milky Way: a cloud of interstellar dust that contains enough matter to create hundreds of new stars. Carina is near the horizon, making its Nebula difficult to see now.

Scorpius is most prominent, high in the **West**. Its brightest star is Antares, which glows a striking red. Far below is Spica, a star in the Virgo constellation. Libra is almost half-way between Antares and Spica. Corvus is about to set below the horizon.

Looking **North-West**, the sky is filled with giant constellations, such as Serpens, Ophiuchus and Hercules, which all lack markers or bright stars. Two constellations that are easy to spot are Corona Borealis (the Northern Crown) and Bootes with Arcturus, its bright orange star.

Meteors

Meteors are bright streaks of light, often called 'shooting stars'. They are caused by sand grains or tiny pebbles, which enter the upper atmosphere at very high speeds. They convert their energy into light and heat, and evaporate completely within a few seconds. They travel near to Earth, and become visible about one or two hundred kilometres away.

Under a dark sky, you can see about a dozen meteors each hour, and even more after midnight. In fact, you may consider these particles as microscopic planets as they all move in orbits around the Sun. The bigger chunks that do not burn up and fall to Earth are called meteorites.

NEW MOON IN AUGUST			
The week around new Moon is ideal for stargazing. An August new Moon will occur:			
Year	**Day**	**Year**	**Day**
2004	16th	2014	25th
2005	5th	2015	14th
2006	23rd	2016	2th
2007	13th	2017	21st
2008	1st & 30th	2018	11th
2009	20th	2019	1st & 30th
2010	10th	2020	19th
2011	29th	2021	8th
2012	17th	2022	27th
2013	6th		

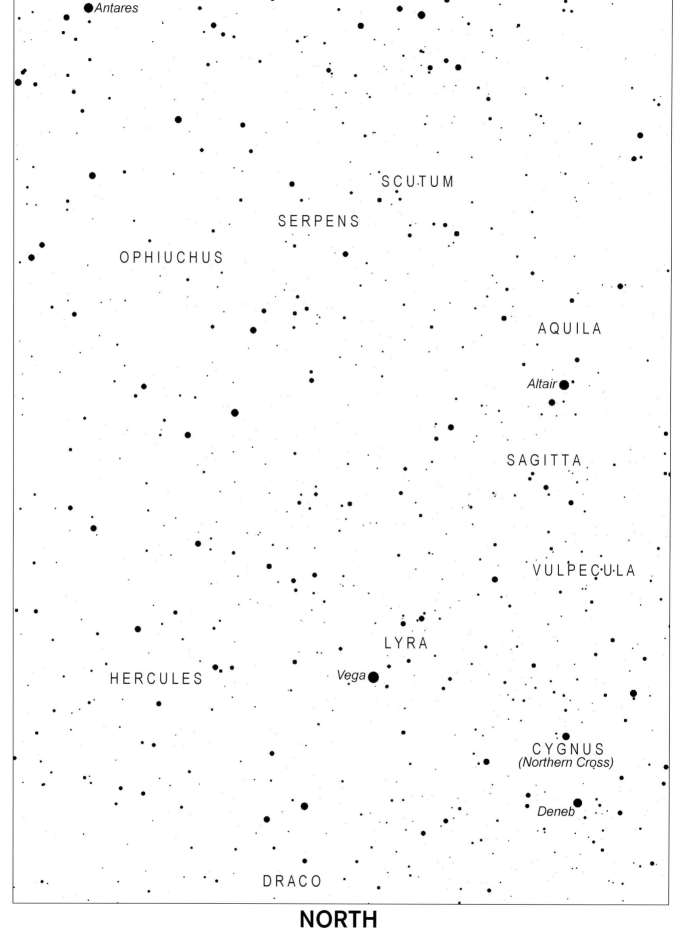

Antares

SCUTUM

SERPENS

OPHIUCHUS

AQUILA

Altair

SAGITTA

VULPECULA

LYRA

Vega

HERCULES

CYGNUS
(Northern Cross)

Deneb

DRACO

NORTH

| | APRIL | | MAY | | JUNE | | JULY | | **AUGUST** | |
| 06h | 05h | 04h | 03h | 02h | 01h | 00h | 23h | 22h | **21h** | 20h |

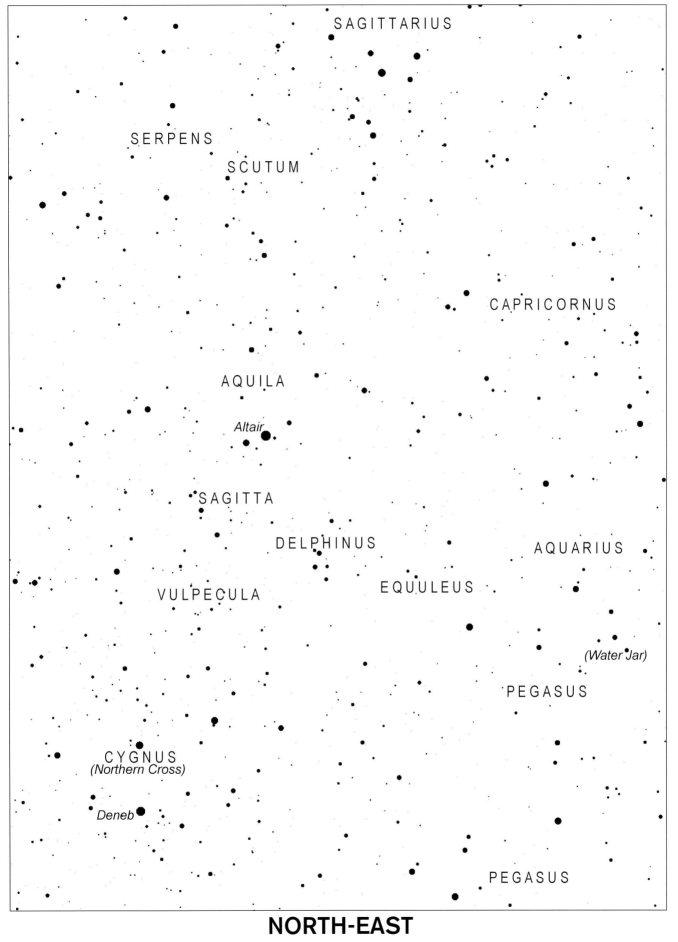

SAGITTARIUS

SERPENS

SCUTUM

CAPRICORNUS

AQUILA

Altair

SAGITTA

DELPHINUS

AQUARIUS

VULPECULA

EQUULEUS

(Water Jar)

PEGASUS

CYGNUS
(Northern Cross)

Deneb

PEGASUS

NORTH-EAST

	APRIL		MAY		JUNE		JULY		**AUGUST**	
06h	05h	04h	03h	02h	01h	00h	23h	22h	**21h**	20h

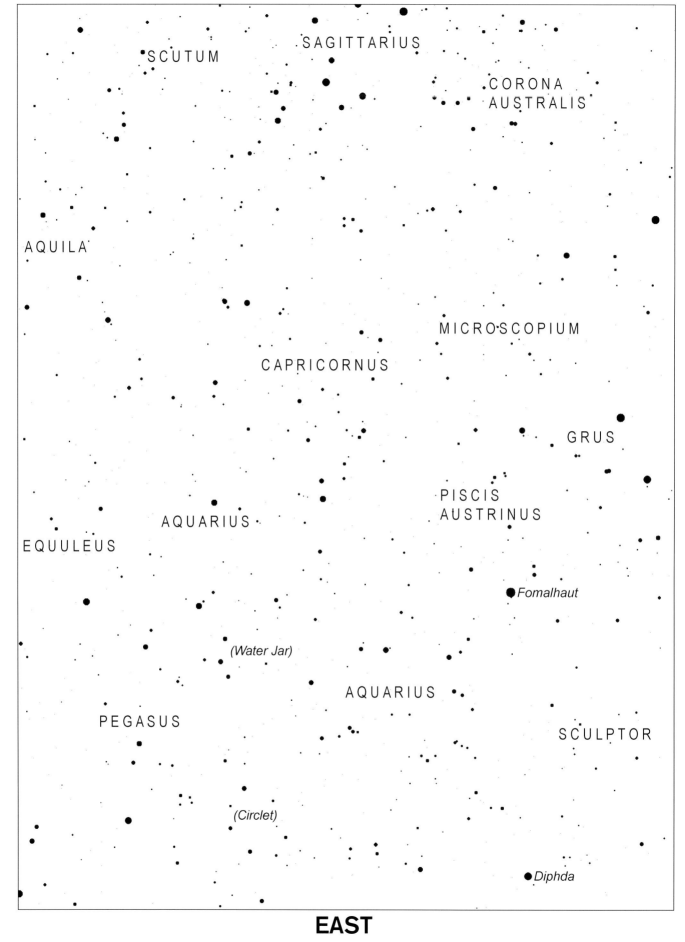

SCUTUM

SAGITTARIUS

CORONA
AUSTRALIS

AQUILA

MICROSCOPIUM

CAPRICORNUS

GRUS

PISCIS
AUSTRINUS

AQUARIUS

EQUULEUS

● *Fomalhaut*

(Water Jar)

AQUARIUS

PEGASUS

SCULPTOR

(Circlet)

● *Diphda*

EAST

	APRIL		MAY		JUNE		JULY		**AUGUST**	
06h	05h	04h	03h	02h	01h	00h	23h	22h	**21h**	20h

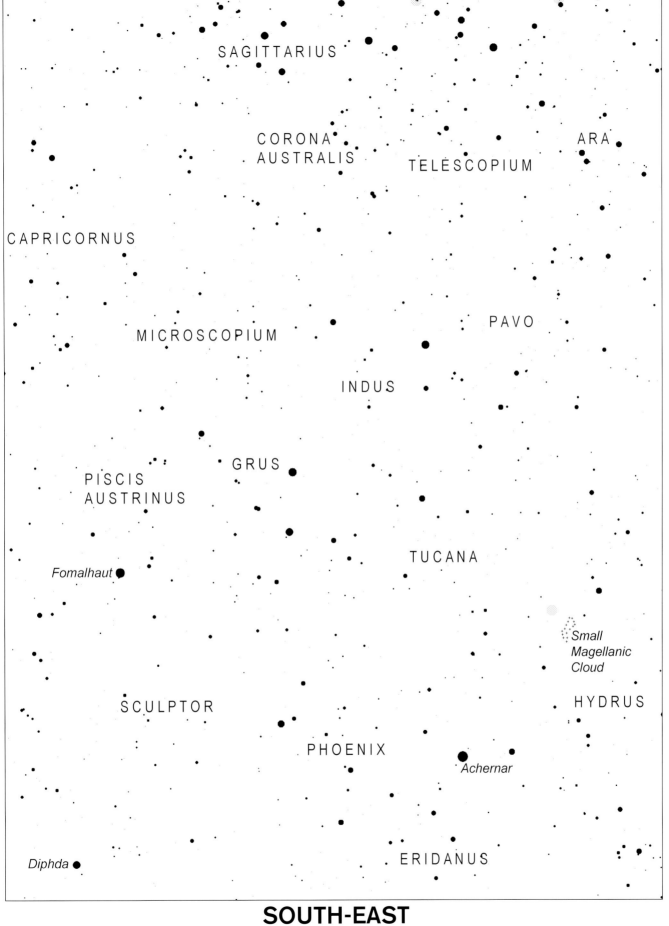

SAGITTARIUS

CORONA
AUSTRALIS

TELESCOPIUM

ARA

CAPRICORNUS

MICROSCOPIUM

PAVO

INDUS

GRUS

PISCIS
AUSTRINUS

TUCANA

Fomalhaut

*Small
Magellanic
Cloud*

SCULPTOR

HYDRUS

PHOENIX

Achernar

ERIDANUS

Diphda

SOUTH-EAST

	APRIL		MAY		JUNE		JULY		**AUGUST**	
06h	05h	04h	03h	02h	01h	00h	23h	22h	**21h**	20h

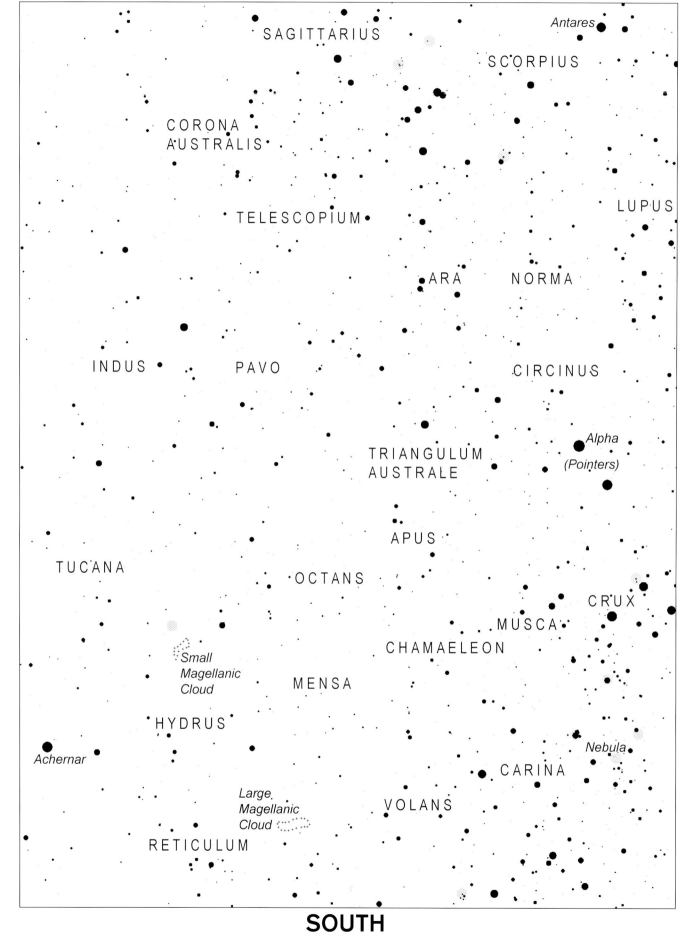

SAGITTARIUS

Antares

SCORPIUS

CORONA
AUSTRALIS

LUPUS

TELESCOPIUM

ARA   NORMA

CIRCINUS

INDUS   PAVO

Alpha
(Pointers)

TRIANGULUM
AUSTRALE

APUS

TUCANA

OCTANS

CRUX

MUSCA

CHAMAELEON

Small
Magellanic
Cloud

MENSA

HYDRUS

Nebula

Achernar

CARINA

Large
Magellanic
Cloud

VOLANS

RETICULUM

SOUTH

APRIL	MAY	JUNE	JULY	**AUGUST**	
06h	05h	04h	03h	02h	01h	00h	23h	22h	**21h**	20h

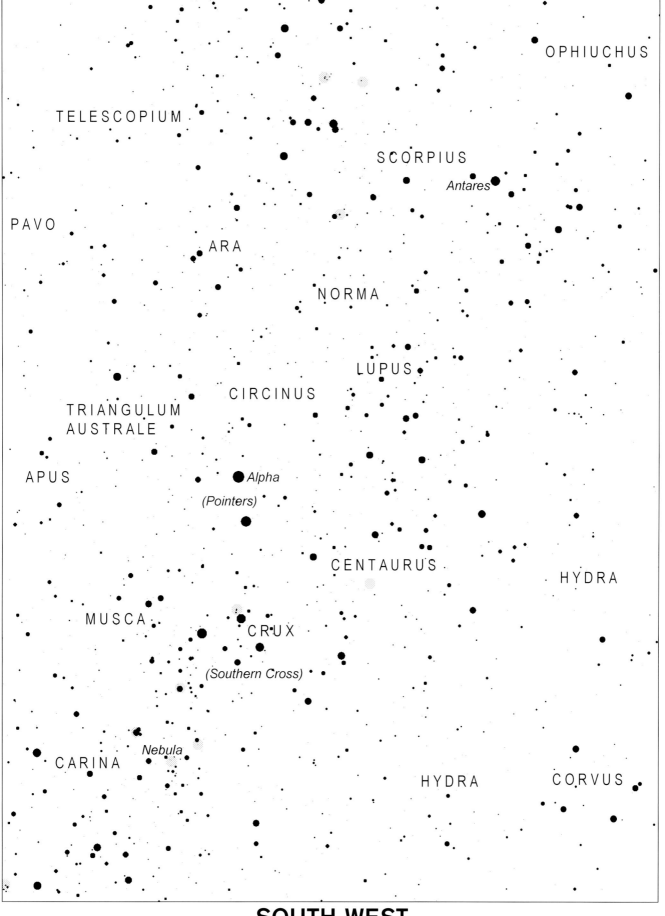

OPHIUCHUS

TELESCOPIUM

SCORPIUS

Antares

PAVO

ARA

NORMA

LUPUS

CIRCINUS

TRIANGULUM
AUSTRALE

APUS

Alpha

(Pointers)

CENTAURUS

HYDRA

MUSCA

CRUX

(Southern Cross)

CARINA   *Nebula*

HYDRA

CORVUS

SOUTH-WEST

APRIL	MAY	JUNE	JULY	**AUGUST**
06h 05h 04h	03h 02h	01h 00h	23h 22h	**21h** 20h

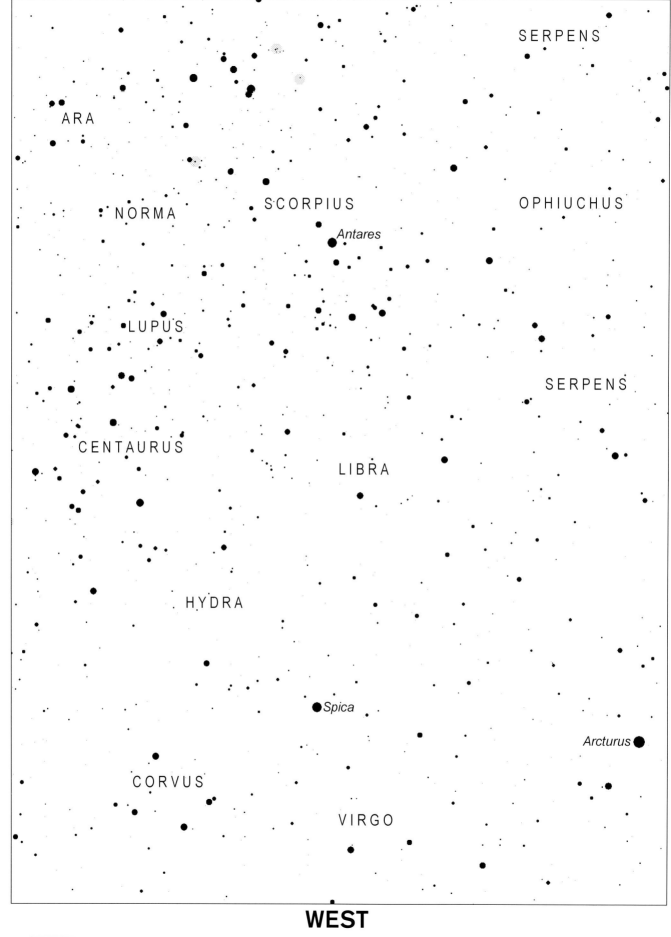

SERPENS

ARA

NORMA

SCORPIUS

OPHIUCHUS

Antares

LUPUS

SERPENS

CENTAURUS

LIBRA

HYDRA

Spica

Arcturus

CORVUS

VIRGO

WEST

	APRIL		MAY		JUNE		JULY		**AUGUST**	
06h	05h	04h	03h	02h	01h	00h	23h	22h	**21h**	20h

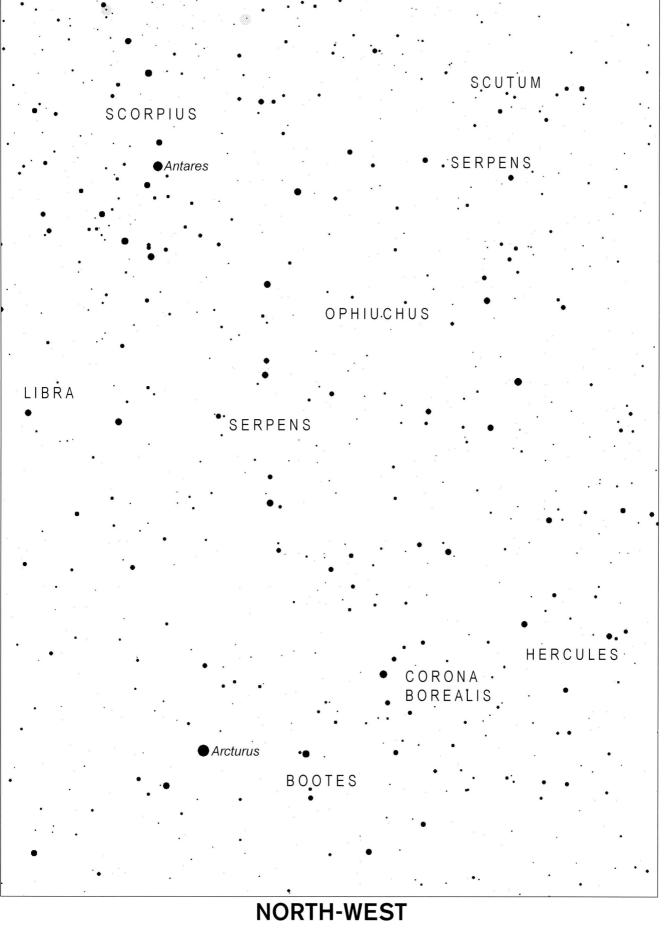

SCUTUM

SCORPIUS

SERPENS

Antares

OPHIUCHUS

LIBRA

SERPENS

HERCULES

CORONA
BOREALIS

Arcturus

BOOTES

NORTH-WEST

APRIL		MAY		JUNE		JULY		**AUGUST**	
06h	05h	04h	03h	02h	01h	00h	23h	22h	**21h**	20h

SET 9
SEPTEMBER AT 21H
USE ALSO IN AUGUST AT 23H, JULY AT 01H, JUNE AT 03H, MAY 05H

AT OTHER TIMES IN SEPTEMBER, USE: SET 10 AT 23H, SET 11 AT 01H, SET 12 AT 03H, SET 1 AT 05H

HIGHLIGHT OF THE SKY TONIGHT

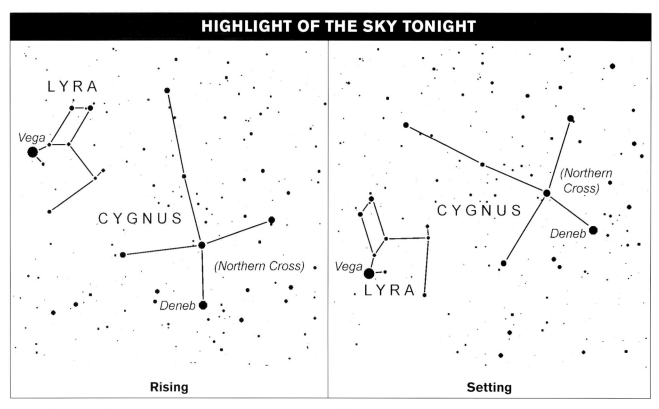

Rising   Setting

Lyra and Cygnus are prominent constellations in Star Maps Set 9. *Observe them quite low in the North.*

A guided tour of the sky

The star Deneb is low in the **North**. It is the brightest star in the Cygnus constellation. In the distant past, some referred to Cygnus as the Northern Cross. To its left is Vega, shining brightly in the constellation of Lyra. Immediately right of Vega is a dim star that binoculars show up as a binary or twin star. Each Twin is itself a binary star, which you can 'split' using a telescope. Much higher, bright Altair shines in the constellation of Aquila, with Sagitta below. Delphinus is visible further down and to the right. Deneb, Vega and Altair are the stars that constitute the Winter Triangle.

Pegasus (the Flying Horse) constellation is visible due **North-East**. The Spring Square forms the bulk of Pegasus. The distorted triangular shape of the constellation of Capricornus is high in the sky. Below Capricornus and to the right is the constellation of Aquarius.

Fomalhaut, the brightest star of Piscis Austrinus, shines high up in the **East**. Much lower is Diphda in the constellation of Cetus. It shines in what appears to be an empty expanse of sky. Pisces is visible near the horizon.

Distinctive Grus constellation is high in the **South-East**. Far below is Achernar, at one end of Eridanus. The Phoenix constellation is higher and to the left of Achernar.

The Magellanic Clouds are in the **South** (two dwarf galaxies lying just outside our Milky Way Galaxy). Although we refer to these galaxies as being 'next door' to ours, their light takes roughly two thousand centuries to reach us. The constellation Pavo is high in the sky, with Triangulum Australe to its lower right side.

The Pointer stars are clearly visible below Triangulum Australe and towards the **South-West**. Using the Pointer stars, you can find Crux (the Southern Cross constellation) low in the sky. The dark lane in the Milky Way divides into two branches near the Norma constellation. The dark lanes are clouds of interstellar dust. High above us shines Corona Australis (the Southern Crown constellation). It is spectacular when seen through binoculars, but it is not a real cluster.

Sagittarius can be seen high in the **West** where the Milky Way is at its brightest. Lower down, the large constellation of Scorpius is prominent, with its curved tail and sting. Red Antares is the brightest star in Scorpius. Use your binoculars to examine a number of bright clusters in Scorpius. The constellation of Libra can be seen right below Antares.

Three huge constellations are spread across the sky in the **North-West**. They are Serpens, Ophiuchus and Hercules and are all difficult to see owing to their lack of bright stars. Little Scutum shows a striking and beautiful Milky Way cloud.

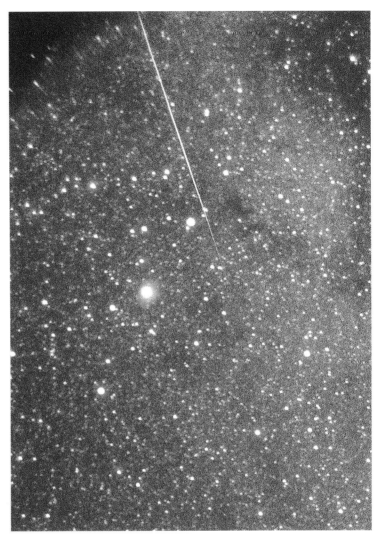

A meteor near Altair

Multiple stars

Stars in multiple systems – in most cases containing two to six stars – have to move in orbits around each other. If they stop, gravity would quickly pull them together to form a single, big star. Because outer space is almost a frictionless vacuum, there is no reason why stars in multiple systems should ever stop moving. No energy is needed to maintain their motion for billions of years.

NEW MOON IN SEPTEMBER

The week around new Moon is ideal for stargazing. A September new Moon will occur:

Year	Day	Year	Day
2004	14th	2014	24th
2005	3rd	2015	13th
2006	22nd	2016	1st
2007	11th	2017	20th
2008	29th	2018	9th
2009	18th	2019	28th
2010	8th	2020	17th
2011	27th	2021	7th
2012	16th	2022	25th
2013	5th		

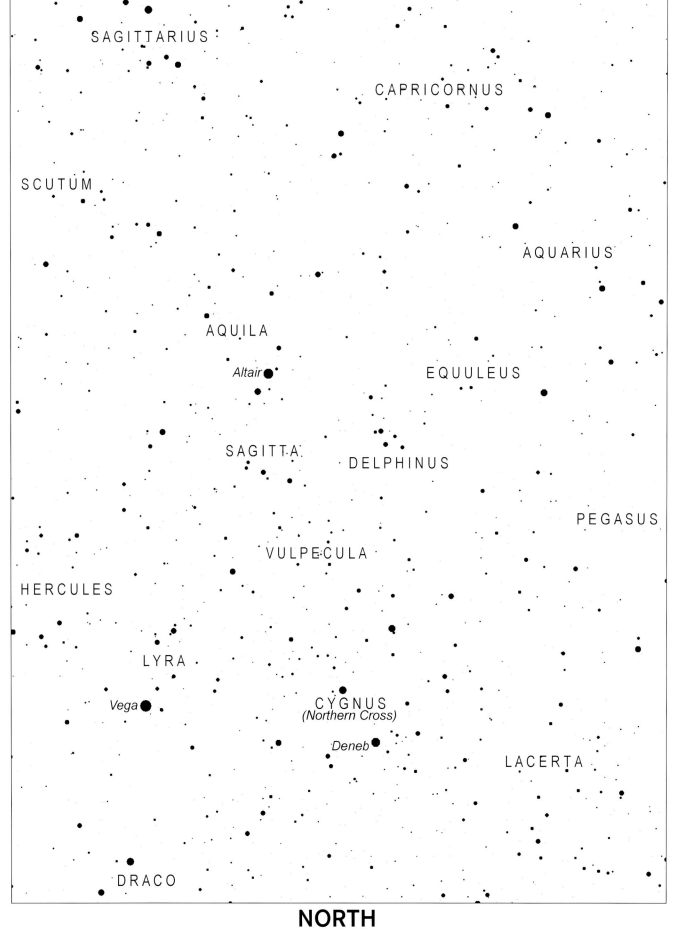

SAGITTARIUS

CAPRICORNUS

SCUTUM

AQUARIUS

AQUILA

Altair

EQUULEUS

SAGITTA

DELPHINUS

PEGASUS

VULPECULA

HERCULES

LYRA

Vega

CYGNUS
(Northern Cross)

Deneb

LACERTA

DRACO

NORTH

MAY	JUNE	JULY	AUGUST	**SEPTEMBER**	
06h	05h	04h	03h	02h	01h	00h	23h	22h	**21h**	20h

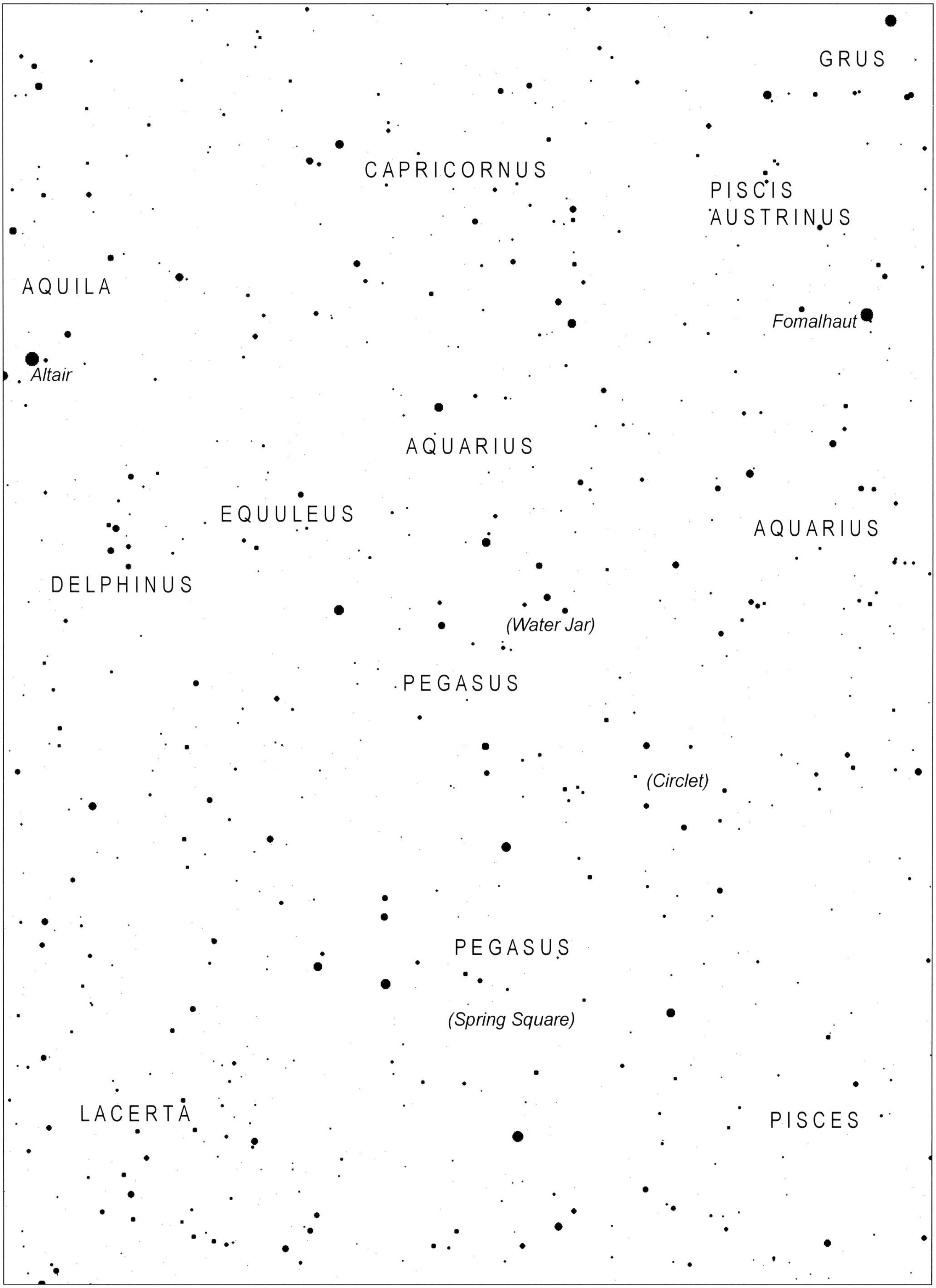

GRUS

CAPRICORNUS

PISCIS
AUSTRINUS

AQUILA

Fomalhaut

Altair

AQUARIUS

EQUULEUS

AQUARIUS

DELPHINUS

(Water Jar)

PEGASUS

(Circlet)

PEGASUS

(Spring Square)

LACERTA

PISCES

NORTH-EAST

	MAY		JUNE		JULY		AUGUST		SEPTEMBER	
06h	05h	04h	03h	02h	01h	00h	23h	22h	**21h**	20h

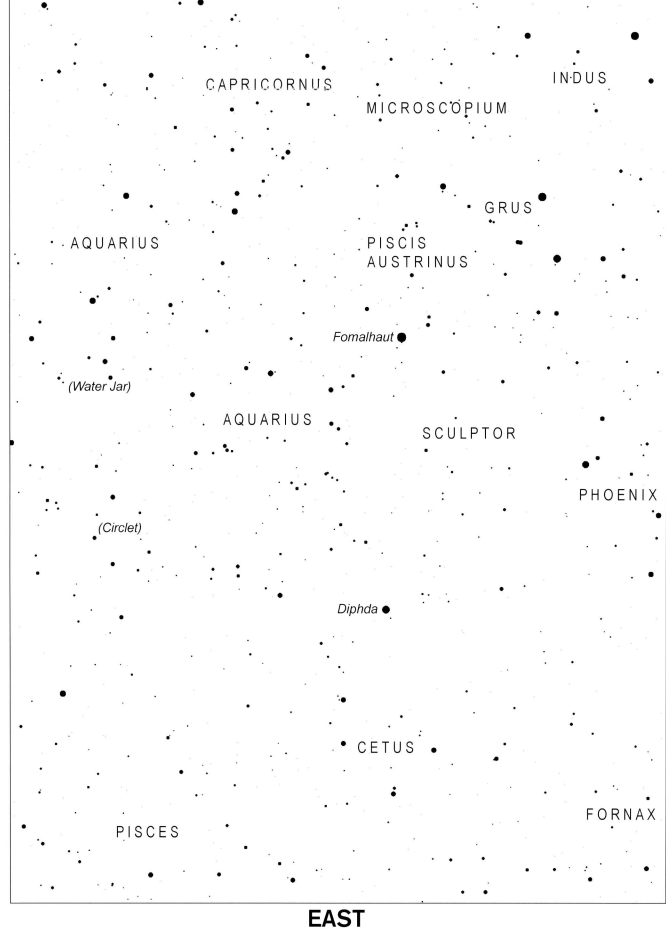

CAPRICORNUS

INDUS

MICROSCOPIUM

GRUS

AQUARIUS

PISCIS
AUSTRINUS

Fomalhaut

(Water Jar)

AQUARIUS

SCULPTOR

PHOENIX

(Circlet)

Diphda

CETUS

FORNAX

PISCES

EAST

	MAY		JUNE		JULY		AUGUST		**SEPTEMBER**	
06h	05h	04h	03h	02h	01h	00h	23h	22h	**21h**	20h

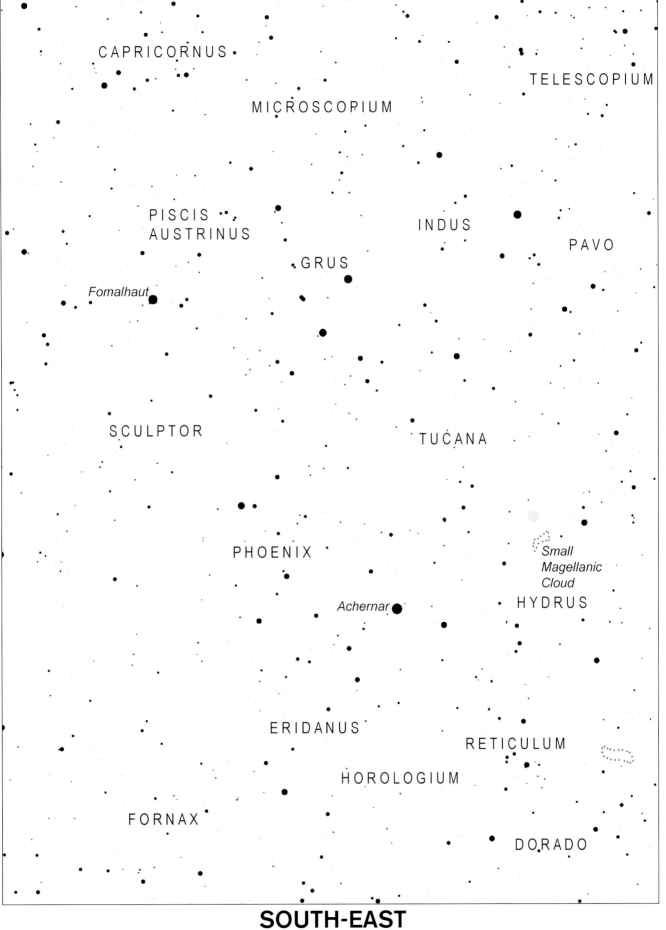

CAPRICORNUS

TELESCOPIUM

MICROSCOPIUM

PISCIS
AUSTRINUS

INDUS

PAVO

GRUS

Fomalhaut

SCULPTOR

TUCANA

*Small
Magellanic
Cloud*

PHOENIX

HYDRUS

Achernar

ERIDANUS

RETICULUM

HOROLOGIUM

FORNAX

DORADO

SOUTH-EAST

	MAY		JUNE		JULY		AUGUST		SEPTEMBER	
06h	05h	04h	03h	02h	01h	00h	23h	22h	**21h**	20h

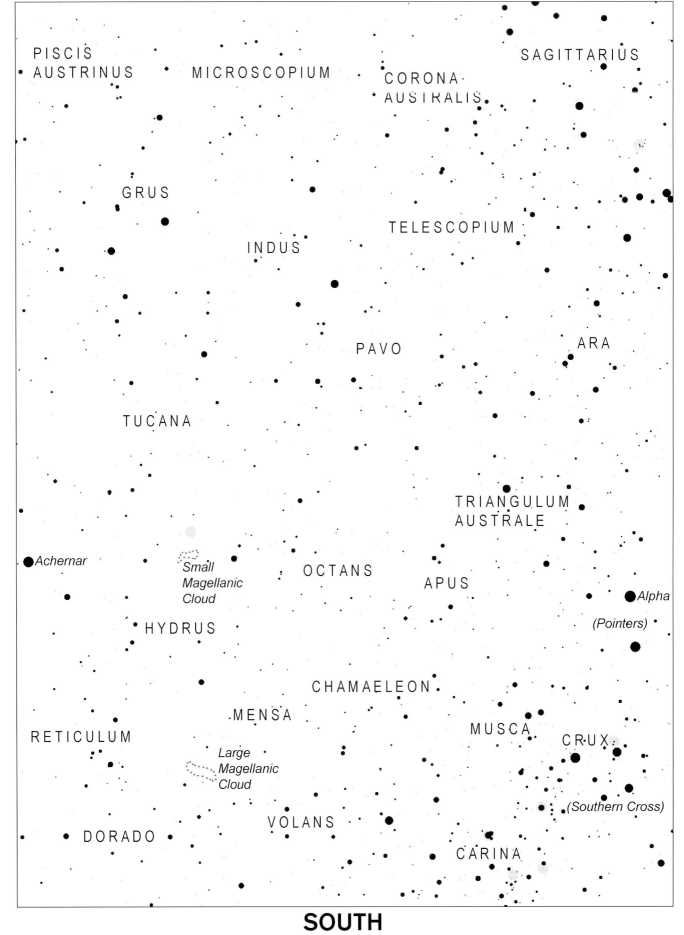

PISCIS
AUSTRINUS

MICROSCOPIUM

CORONA
AUSTRALIS

SAGITTARIUS

GRUS

TELESCOPIUM

INDUS

PAVO

ARA

TUCANA

TRIANGULUM
AUSTRALE

Achernar

*Small
Magellanic
Cloud*

OCTANS

APUS

Alpha

(Pointers)

HYDRUS

CHAMAELEON

MENSA

MUSCA

CRUX

RETICULUM

*Large
Magellanic
Cloud*

(Southern Cross)

VOLANS

DORADO

CARINA

SOUTH

	MAY		JUNE		JULY		AUGUST		SEPTEMBER	
06h	05h	04h	03h	02h	01h	00h	23h	22h	**21h**	20h

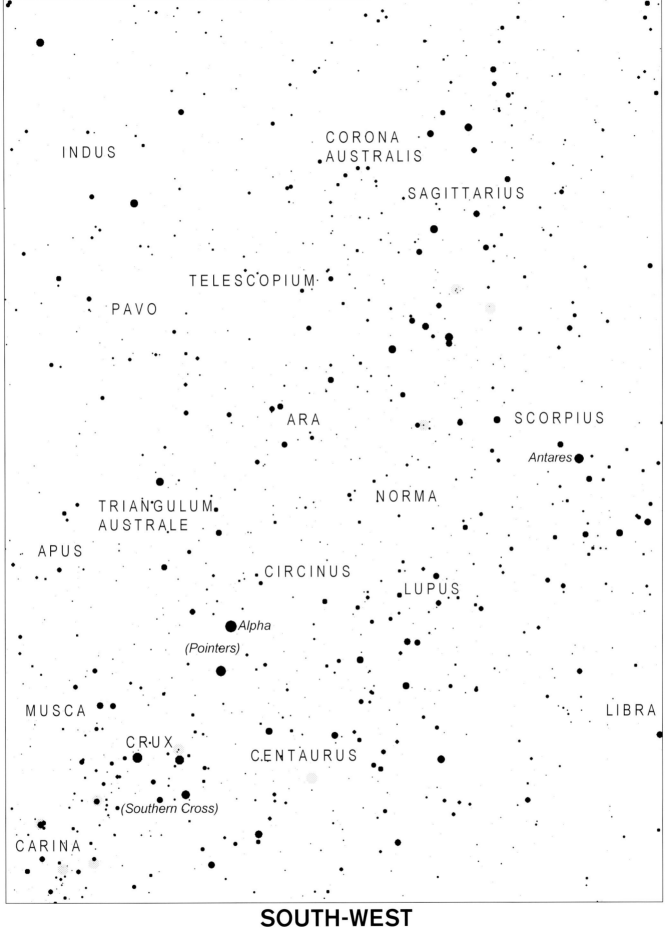

INDUS

CORONA
AUSTRALIS

SAGITTARIUS

TELESCOPIUM

PAVO

ARA

SCORPIUS

Antares

TRIANGULUM
AUSTRALE

NORMA

APUS

CIRCINUS

LUPUS

Alpha

(Pointers)

MUSCA

LIBRA

CRUX

CENTAURUS

(Southern Cross)

CARINA

SOUTH-WEST

| | MAY | | JUNE | | JULY | | AUGUST | | **SEPTEMBER** | |
| 06h | 05h | 04h | 03h | 02h | 01h | 00h | 23h | 22h | **21h** | 20h |

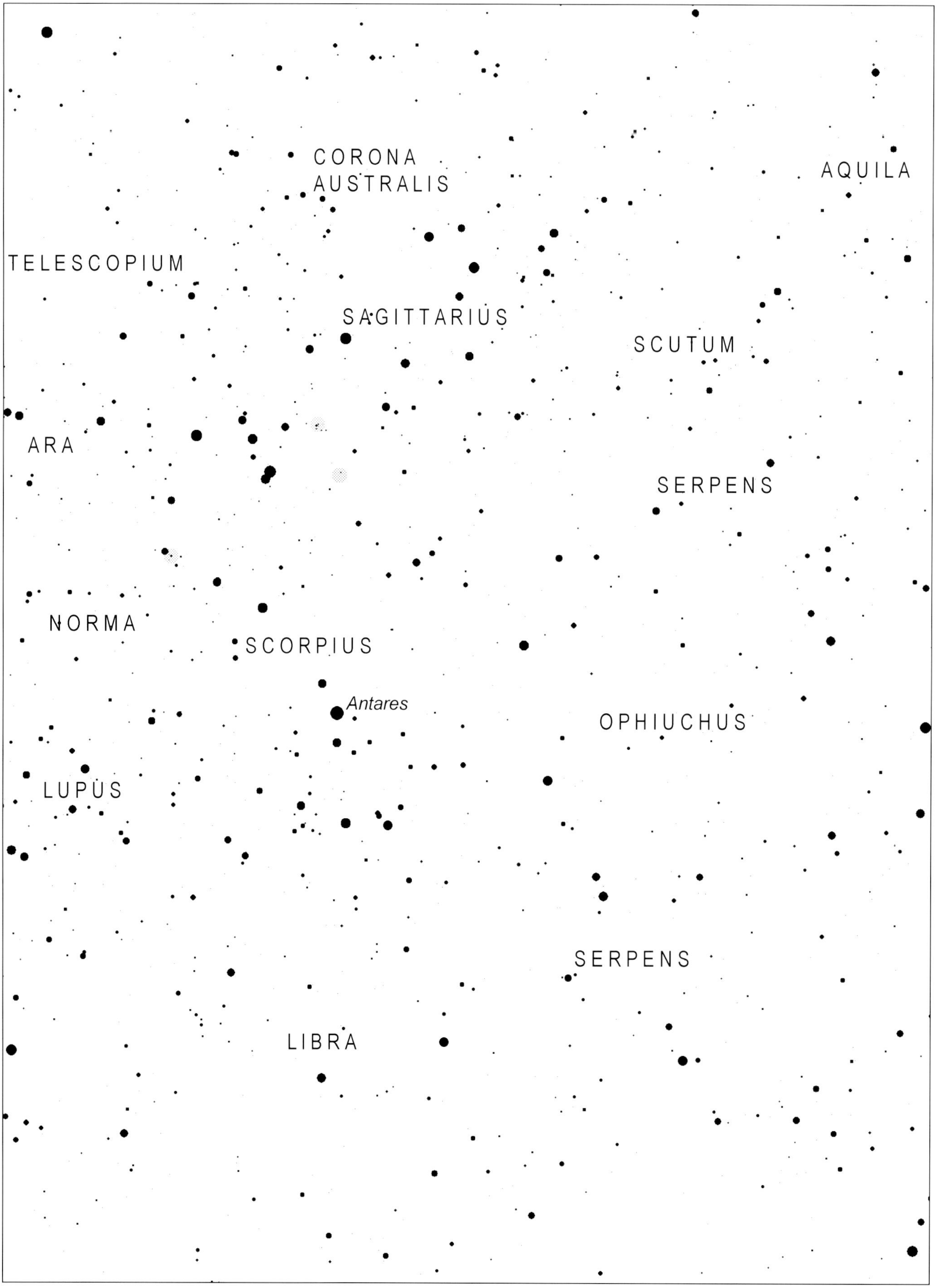

CORONA
AUSTRALIS

AQUILA

TELESCOPIUM

SAGITTARIUS

SCUTUM

ARA

SERPENS

NORMA

SCORPIUS

Antares

OPHIUCHUS

LUPUS

SERPENS

LIBRA

WEST

	MAY		JUNE		JULY		AUGUST		**SEPTEMBER**	
06h	05h	04h	03h	02h	01h	00h	23h	22h	**21h**	20h

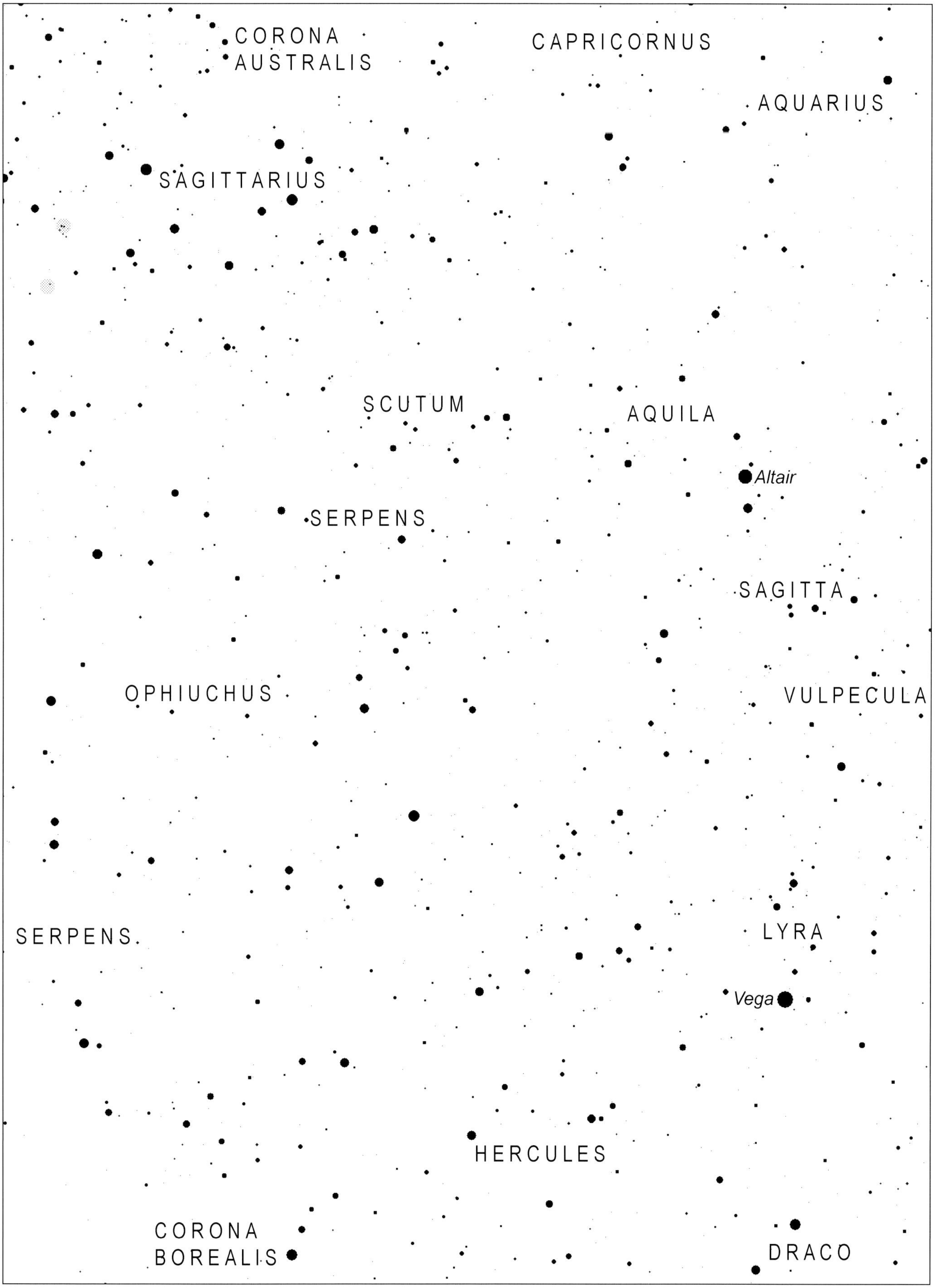

CORONA
AUSTRALIS

CAPRICORNUS

AQUARIUS

SAGITTARIUS

SCUTUM

AQUILA

● *Altair*

SERPENS

SAGITTA

VULPECULA

OPHIUCHUS

SERPENS.

LYRA

Vega ●

HERCULES

CORONA
BOREALIS ●

DRACO

NORTH-WEST

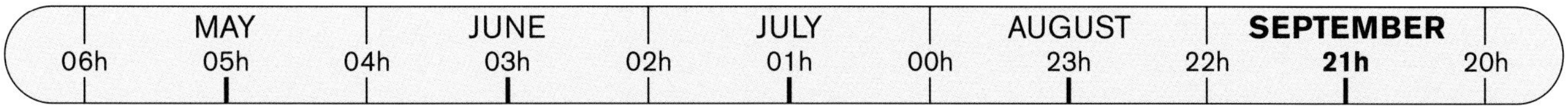

SET 10
OCTOBER AT 21H

USE ALSO IN SEPTEMBER AT 23H, AUGUST AT 01H, JULY AT 03H, JUNE AT 05H

AT OTHER TIMES IN OCTOBER, USE: SET 11 AT 23H, SET 12 AT 01H, SET 1 AT 03H, AND SET 2 AT 05H

HIGHLIGHT OF THE SKY TONIGHT

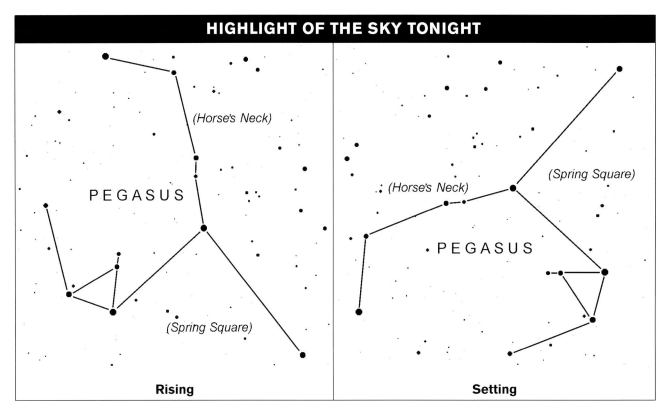

Rising | Setting

Pegasus with its Spring Square is a prominent constellation in Star Maps Set 10. *Observe it quite high in the North.*

A guided tour of the sky

Pegasus (the Flying Horse) constellation is high in the **North**. It is large but lacks really bright stars. However, the four stars that make up its Spring Square can be easily identified. Directly above the Horse's Neck is the Water Jar of Aquarius, while the Circlet of stars (at one end of Pisces) can be seen lying well above the Square.

The constellation of Andromeda is connected to Pegasus and is visible in the **North-East**. It contains the Andromeda Galaxy, which bears a strong resemblance to our own galaxy. It is, without doubt, the most remote object that we can see with the naked eye; its faint light travels a few million years to reach us. Two constellations, Triangulum and Aries, are visible to the right of Andromeda. Pisces is shaped like a faint and tilted 'V', and can be seen directly above Triangulum and Aries.

Fomalhaut shines brightly, high up in the **East**. Lower in the sky, Diphda is visible in the constellation of Cetus, where the sky appears to be relatively devoid of stars. Quite low you can see two 'twists' in the 'river' Eridanus.

Achernar is the bright star at one end of the Eridanus 'river'. It shines high in the **South-East**. The Phoenix constellation lies above Achernar, to its left. Bright Canopus stands out near the horizon. Canopus appears

Nuclear fuel

We can see a star because it is hot and radiates energy. If it stopped burning, it would quickly cool down and start to contract. As long as a star has plenty of nuclear fuel, it will maintain its struggle against gravity. However, when the fuel depletes, the final collapse of a star is inevitable.

The Orion Nebula (left) with Orion's Belt (right)

to lie almost along a line with Fomalhaut and Achernar.

The striking constellation of Grus is high up in the **South**. Below it, the constellation of Tucana is hard to identify. Still lower are the Magellanic Clouds, two dwarf galaxies that are a dozen times nearer to us than the Andromeda Galaxy. Some details of these closer galaxies are visible through binoculars, but some of their brightest individual stars can only be seen through a telescope.

The Pointer stars are low, towards the **South-West**. Directly above them is the constellation of Triangulum Australe, with the Ara constellation to its right. Further right, the beautiful constellation of Scorpius stands out. Red Antares is its brightest star. Use binoculars to examine some fine clusters in the Scorpius constellation.

Sagittarius is further **West**, in the brightest part of the Milky Way, which is a wonderful spectacle. A little higher and to the left, Corona Australis is an interesting sight. Much higher, the distorted triangle of Capricornus can be seen. Below it is the constellation of Scutum, with its pretty Milky Way cloud.

Looking **North-West**, you can see the star Altair in Aquila, with constellations Delphinus to its right and Sagitta just below. These two small constellations look impressive through binoculars. Very bright Vega is about to set below the horizon. The star Deneb in Cygnus will set about one hour afterwards.

A star's struggle for survival

A star is a glowing, hot ball of gases. Why is it that a star has to be hot? To survive, it must counter its own gravity and, in order to do this, a strong outward gas pressure is required. This pressure is created and a balance maintained through the burning of nuclear fuel to keep its internal temperatures high.

NEW MOON IN OCTOBER

The week around new Moon is ideal for stargazing. An October new Moon will occur:

Year	Day	Year	Day
2004	14th	2014	23rd
2005	3rd	2015	13th
2006	22nd	2016	1st & 30th
2007	11th	2017	19th
2008	29th	2018	9th
2009	18th	2019	28th
2010	7th	2020	16th
2011	26th	2021	6th
2012	15th	2022	25th
2013	5th		

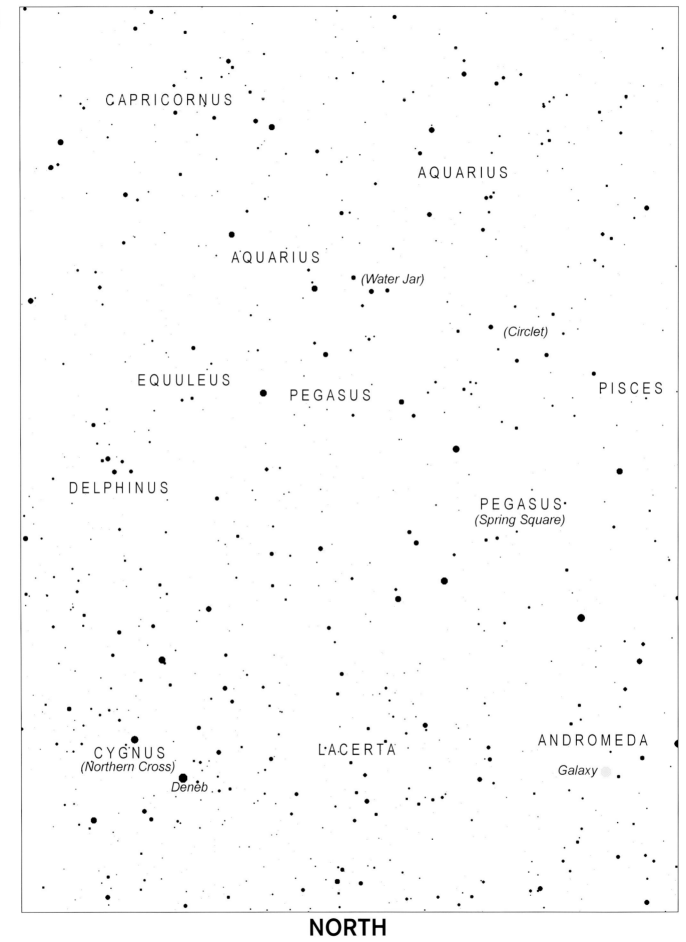

CAPRICORNUS

AQUARIUS

AQUARIUS

(Water Jar)

(Circlet)

EQUULEUS

PEGASUS

PISCES

DELPHINUS

PEGASUS
(Spring Square)

CYGNUS
(Northern Cross)

LACERTA

ANDROMEDA

Galaxy

Deneb

NORTH

JUNE	JULY	AUGUST	SEPTEMBER	**OCTOBER**	
06h	05h	04h	03h	02h	01h	00h	23h	22h	**21h**	20h

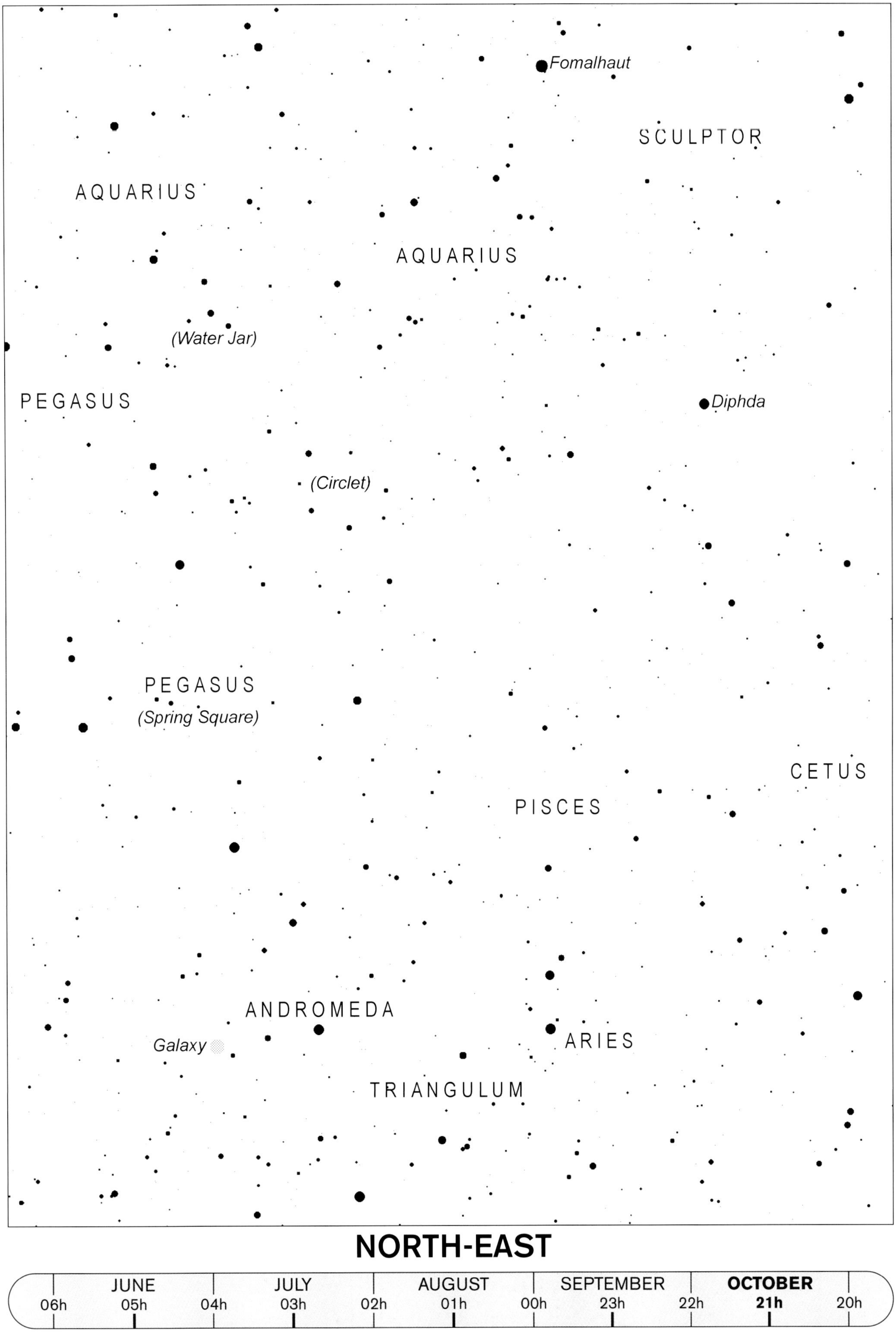

Fomalhaut

SCULPTOR

AQUARIUS

AQUARIUS

(Water Jar)

PEGASUS

Diphda

(Circlet)

PEGASUS
(Spring Square)

CETUS

PISCES

ANDROMEDA

Galaxy

ARIES

TRIANGULUM

NORTH-EAST

	JUNE		JULY		AUGUST		SEPTEMBER		**OCTOBER**	
06h	05h	04h	03h	02h	01h	00h	23h	22h	**21h**	20h

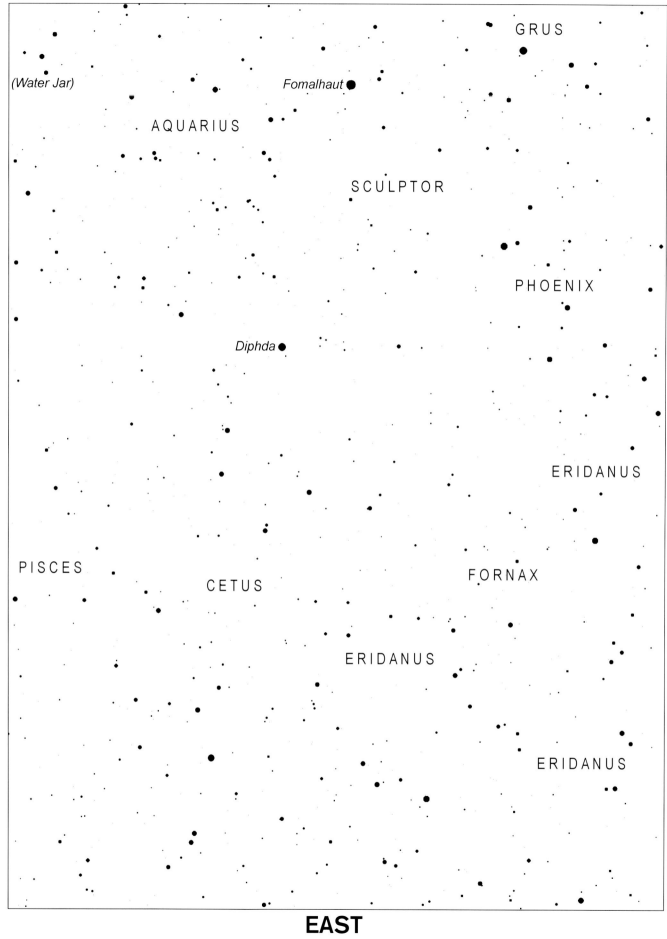

GRUS

(Water Jar)

Fomalhaut

AQUARIUS

SCULPTOR

PHOENIX

Diphda

ERIDANUS

PISCES

CETUS

FORNAX

ERIDANUS

ERIDANUS

EAST

JUNE	JULY	AUGUST	SEPTEMBER	**OCTOBER**
06h 05h 04h	03h 02h	01h 00h	23h 22h	**21h** 20h

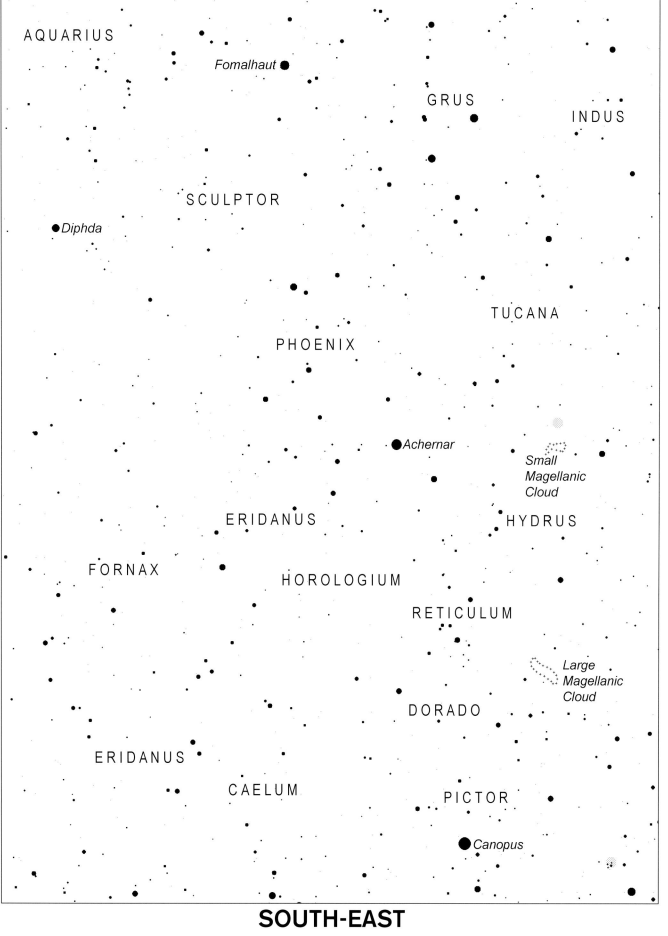

AQUARIUS

Fomalhaut ●

GRUS

INDUS

SCULPTOR

● *Diphda*

TUCANA

PHOENIX

● *Achernar*

Small
Magellanic
Cloud

ERIDANUS

HYDRUS

FORNAX

HOROLOGIUM

RETICULUM

Large
Magellanic
Cloud

DORADO

ERIDANUS

CAELUM

PICTOR

● *Canopus*

SOUTH-EAST

	JUNE		JULY		AUGUST		SEPTEMBER		OCTOBER	
06h	05h	04h	03h	02h	01h	00h	23h	22h	**21h**	20h

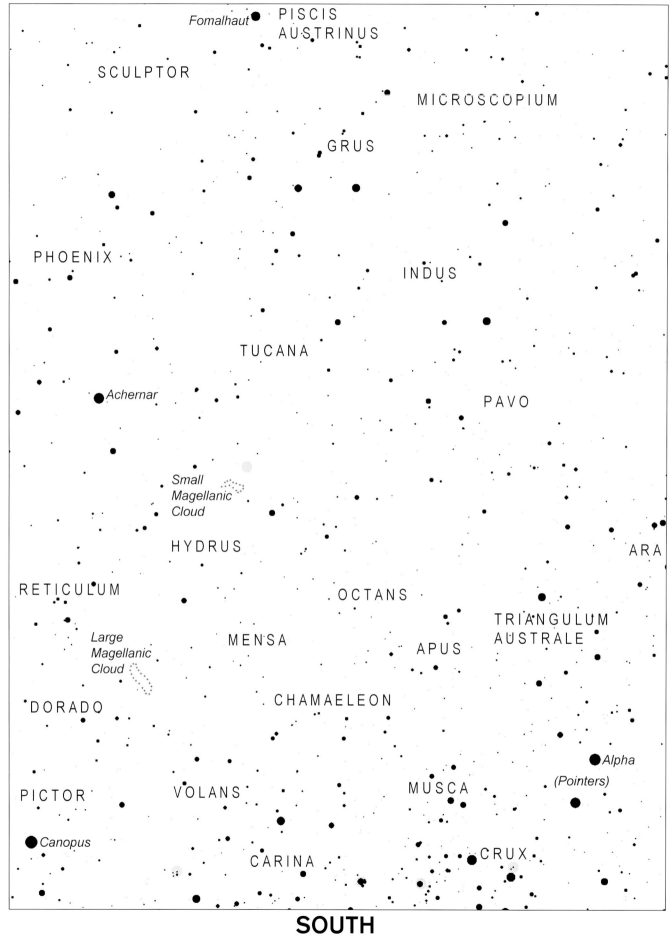

Fomalhaut

PISCIS
AUSTRINUS

SCULPTOR

MICROSCOPIUM

GRUS

PHOENIX

INDUS

TUCANA

PAVO

Achernar

Small
Magellanic
Cloud

HYDRUS

ARA

RETICULUM

OCTANS

TRIANGULUM
AUSTRALE

Large
Magellanic
Cloud

MENSA

APUS

CHAMAELEON

DORADO

Alpha
(Pointers)

PICTOR

VOLANS

MUSCA

Canopus

CARINA

CRUX

SOUTH

	JUNE		JULY		AUGUST		SEPTEMBER		OCTOBER	
06h	05h	04h	03h	02h	01h	00h	23h	22h	21h	20h

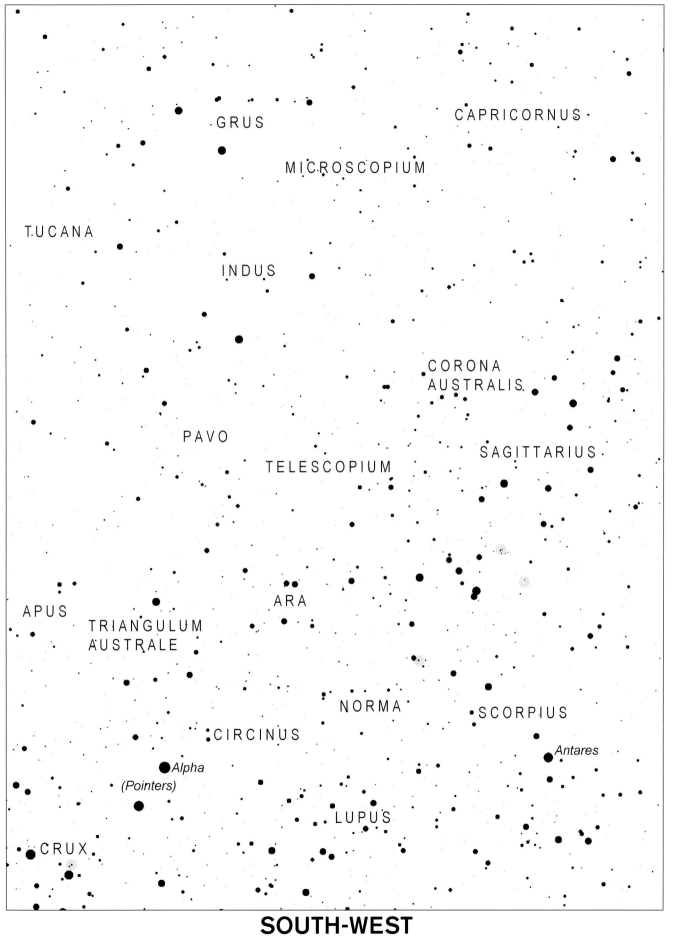

GRUS

CAPRICORNUS

MICROSCOPIUM

TUCANA

INDUS

CORONA
AUSTRALIS

PAVO

SAGITTARIUS

TELESCOPIUM

APUS

ARA

TRIANGULUM
AUSTRALE

NORMA

SCORPIUS

CIRCINUS

Antares

Alpha
(Pointers)

LUPUS

CRUX

SOUTH-WEST

	JUNE		JULY		AUGUST		SEPTEMBER		**OCTOBER**	
06h	05h	04h	03h	02h	01h	00h	23h	22h	**21h**	20h

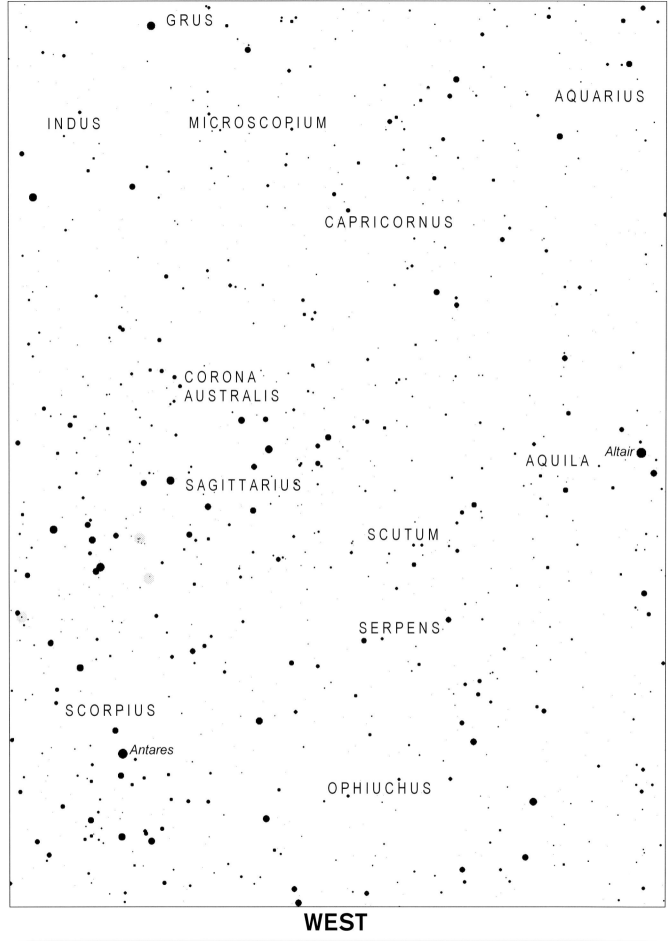

GRUS

AQUARIUS

INDUS   MICROSCOPIUM

CAPRICORNUS

CORONA
AUSTRALIS

AQUILA   *Altair*

SAGITTARIUS

SCUTUM

SERPENS

SCORPIUS

Antares

OPHIUCHUS

WEST

	JUNE		JULY		AUGUST		SEPTEMBER		**OCTOBER**	
06h	05h	04h	03h	02h	01h	00h	23h	22h	**21h**	20h

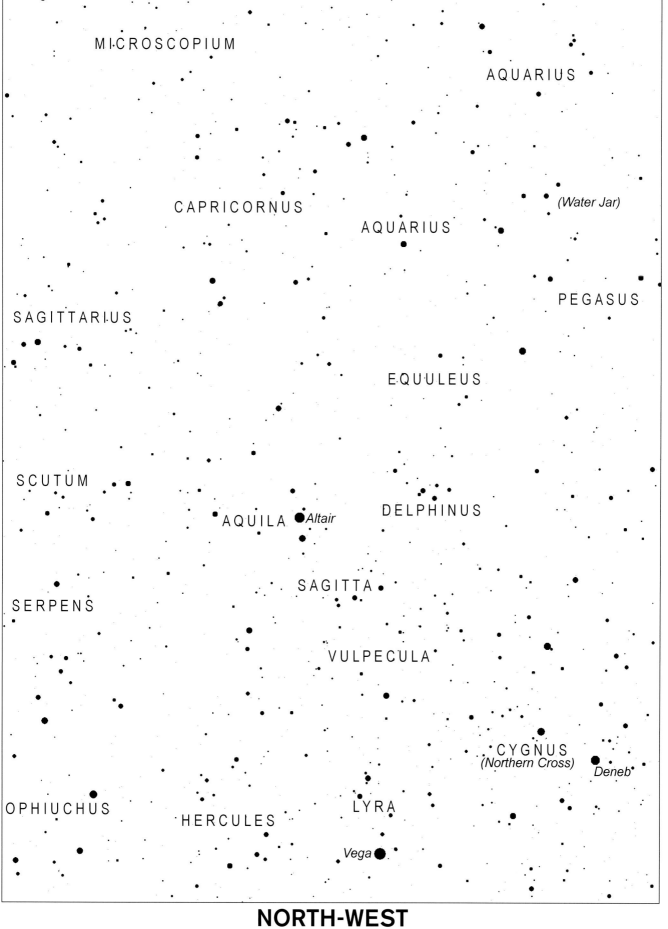

MICROSCOPIUM

AQUARIUS

CAPRICORNUS

AQUARIUS

(Water Jar)

PEGASUS

SAGITTARIUS

EQUULEUS

SCUTUM

AQUILA *Altair*

DELPHINUS

SAGITTA

SERPENS

VULPECULA

OPHIUCHUS

HERCULES

LYRA

CYGNUS
(Northern Cross)

Deneb

Vega

NORTH-WEST

| 06h | JUNE 05h | 04h | JULY 03h | 02h | AUGUST 01h | 00h | SEPTEMBER 23h | 22h | OCTOBER 21h | 20h |

SET 11
NOVEMBER AT 21H

USE ALSO IN OCTOBER AT 23H, SEPTEMBER AT 01H, AUGUST AT 03H, JULY AT 05H

AT OTHER TIMES IN NOVEMBER, USE: SET 12 AT 23H, SET 1 AT 01H, AND SET 2 AT 03H

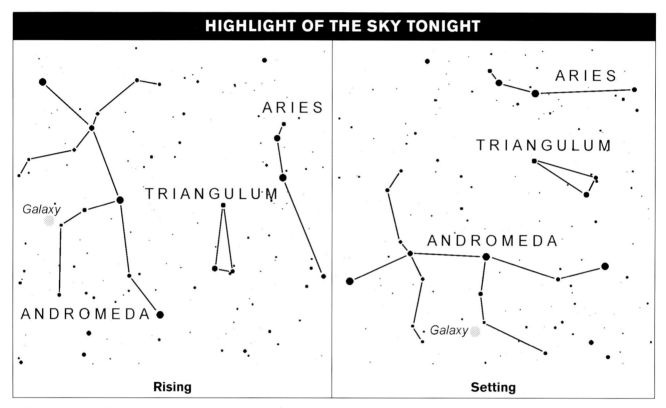

HIGHLIGHT OF THE SKY TONIGHT

Rising

Setting

Aries, Andromeda and Triangulum are prominent constellations in Star Maps Set 11. *Observe them low in the North.*

A guided tour of the sky

The horizon now coincides with the plane of our galaxy's 'disk'. Consequently, the Milky Way is low in every direction, and the sky's summit seems to be devoid of stars. The night sky reveals that the Milky Way Galaxy is not spherical but is a flat disk (like many other galaxies). Galaxies become this shape through the interplay of gravity and rotation. The Sun and its neighbours orbit near the edge of the Milky Way Galaxy so fast that they cover a few hundred kilometres each second. Yet it takes each star a few hundred million years to complete just one orbit, because our galaxy is so huge.

Looking **North**, you can see the constellation of Pegasus with the four stars of the Spring Square. It points the way to the constellation Andromeda, which contains our neighbouring galaxy, visible to the naked eye as a distant blur. You may see the Andromeda Galaxy better through binoculars.

In the **North-East**, the constellation of Cetus fills a large part of the sky. All the stars in this constellation are dim, except the one named Diphda. Very low in the sky are two star clusters, the Pleiades and the Hyades in the Taurus constellation. They are real beauties when seen through binoculars.

The Milky Way

Our galaxy holds enough stars to give everyone on Earth a star for each birthday of their lives, although fewer than nine thousand of these stars are visible to the naked eye. Depending on its size, a telescope may reveal several million stars.

The Small Magellanic Cloud

Shining low in the **East** is the splendid Orion constellation. See how blue Rigel contrasts with red Betelgeuse. Near Orion's Belt (three stars in a row) is the famous Nebula. Bright Sirius is visible to the right and is so close to the horizon that its vivid twinkling may frighten the naïve observer.

Low in the **South-East**, you can see Canopus. Far above is Achernar, indicating one end of the huge, meandering 'river' Eridanus. The other end of Eridanus is near Rigel in Orion.

Looking **South**, the Magellanic Clouds are easily spotted with the naked eye. These dwarf galaxies are a dozen times nearer to Earth than the Andromeda Galaxy. The two Pointers are almost on the horizon.

In the **South-West**, the constellation of Grus can be seen, high up. Far below, you can see the constellation of Corona Australis. To the right of Corona Australis and lower in the sky, the constellation of Sagittarius is easy to identify.

High up and due **West**, bright Fomalhaut shines in Piscis Austrinus. Directly below Piscis Austrinus, you can see the distorted triangle of Capricornus. Altair is a very bright star and can be seen diagonally to the right and far below Capricornus.

Aquarius is hard to identify, but it can be seen high in the **North-West**, above and to the left of the 'neck' of Pegasus. The small constellation of Delphinus, to the right of Altair, is easy to spot.

Neighbouring galaxies

There may be as many galaxies in the Universe as there are stars in our own galaxy. However, only three galaxies are visible to the naked eye: the two Magellanic Clouds and the Andromeda Galaxy, which is the same size as our own, but a dozen times farther away than the two Magellanic Clouds. The Andromeda Galaxy bears a visual resemblance to our own. Its light travels a few million years to reach the Earth.

NEW MOON IN NOVEMBER

The week around new Moon is ideal for stargazing. A November new Moon will occur:

Year	Day	Year	Day
2004	12th	2014	22nd
2005	2nd	2015	11th
2006	21st	2016	29th
2007	10th	2017	18th
2008	27th	2018	7th
2009	16th	2019	26th
2010	6th	2020	15th
2011	25th	2021	4th
2012	14th	2022	24th
2013	3rd		

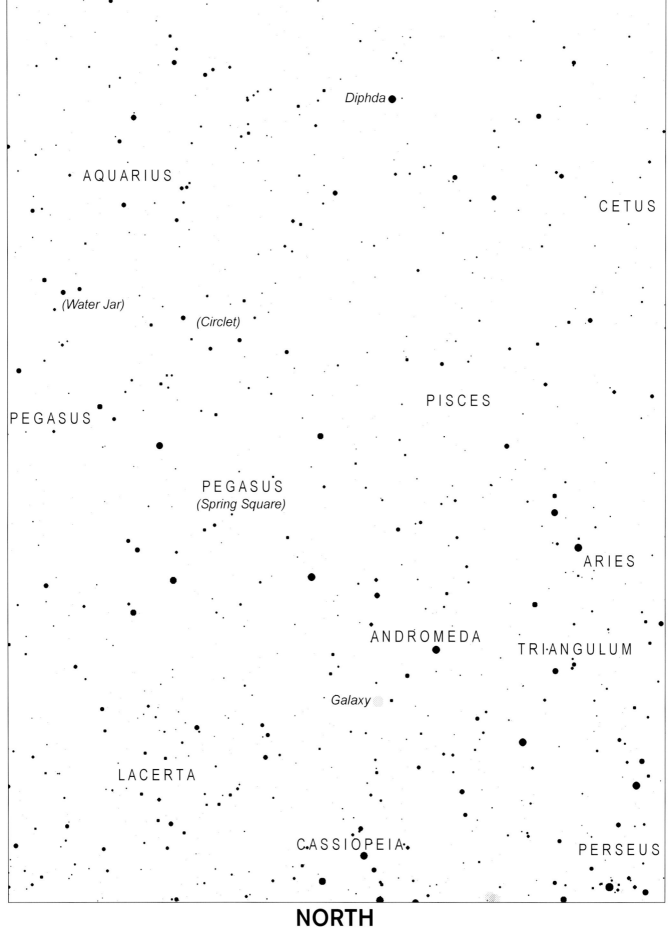

Diphda

AQUARIUS

CETUS

(Water Jar)

(Circlet)

PISCES

PEGASUS

PEGASUS
(Spring Square)

ARIES

ANDROMEDA

TRIANGULUM

Galaxy

LACERTA

CASSIOPEIA

PERSEUS

NORTH

JULY	AUGUST	SEPTEMBER	OCTOBER	**NOVEMBER**
06h 05h 04h	03h 02h	01h 00h	23h 22h	**21h** 20h

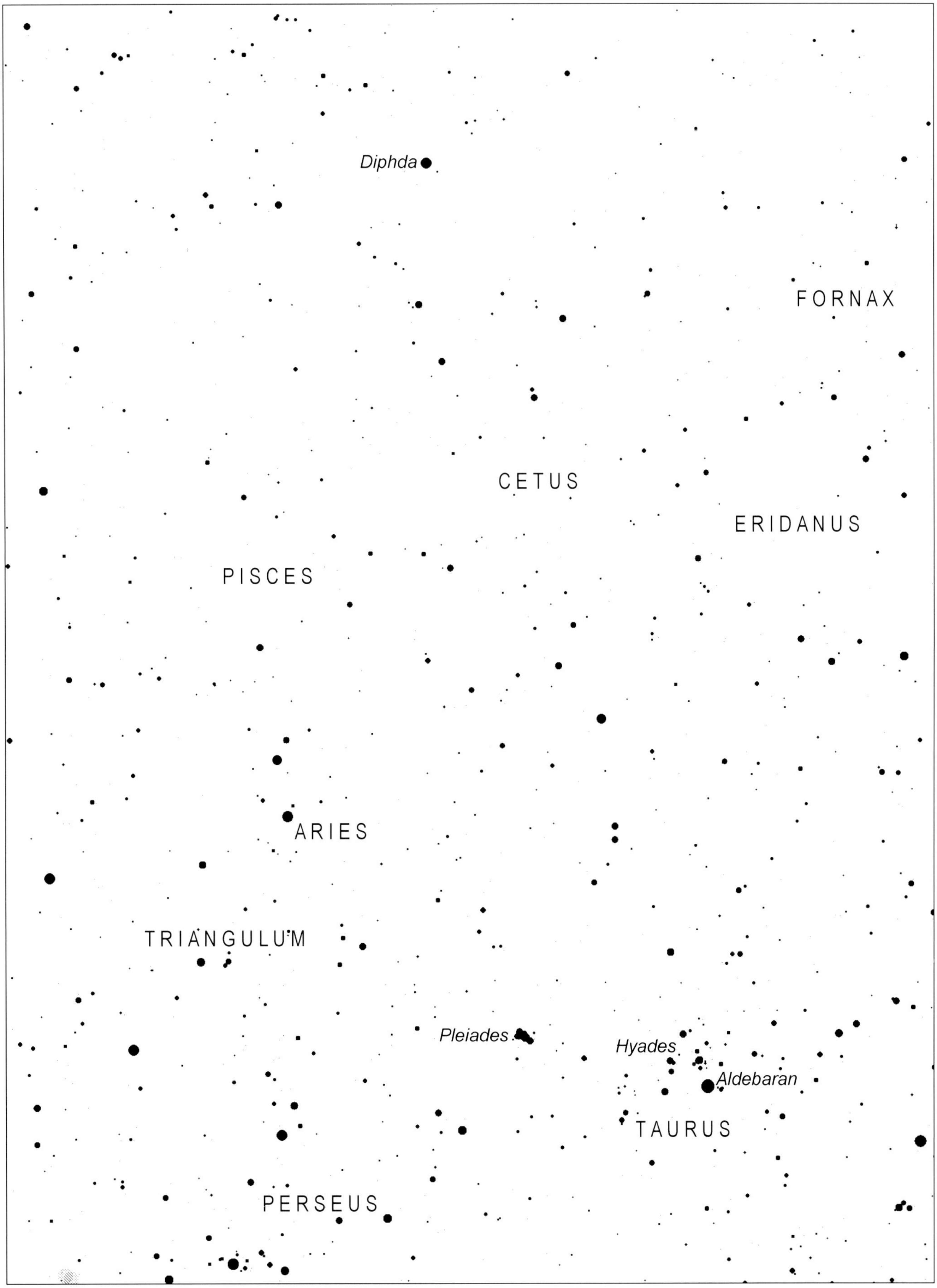

Diphda ●

FORNAX

CETUS

ERIDANUS

PISCES

ARIES

TRIANGULUM

Pleiades

Hyades

Aldebaran

TAURUS

PERSEUS

NORTH-EAST

	JULY		AUGUST		SEPTEMBER		OCTOBER		**NOVEMBER**	
06h	05h	04h	03h	02h	01h	00h	23h	22h	**21h**	20h

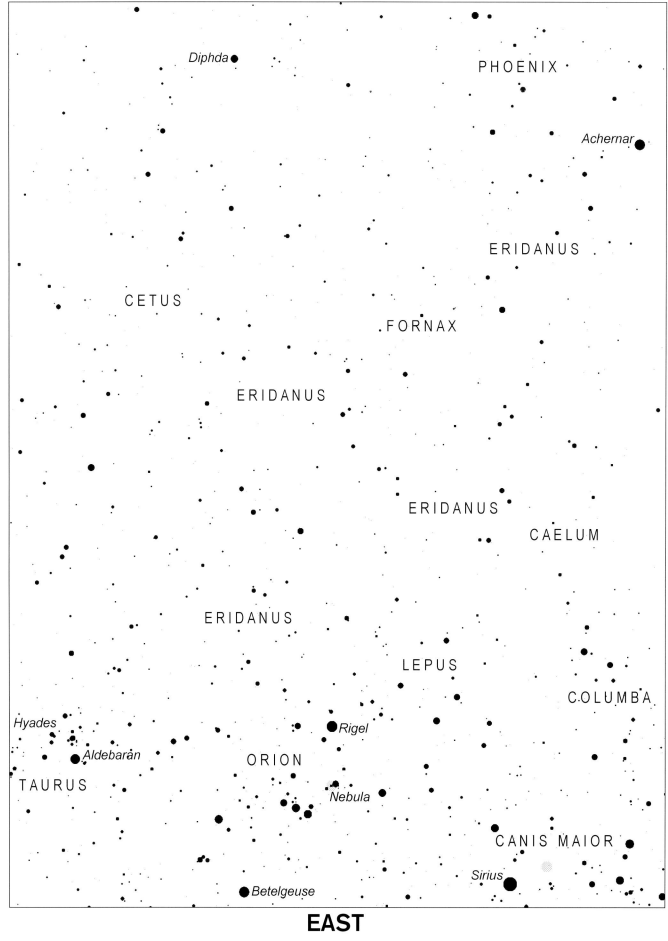

Diphda

PHOENIX

Achernar

ERIDANUS

CETUS

FORNAX

ERIDANUS

ERIDANUS

CAELUM

ERIDANUS

LEPUS

COLUMBA

Hyades

Rigel

Aldebaran

ORION

TAURUS

Nebula

CANIS MAIOR

Sirius

Betelgeuse

EAST

	JULY		AUGUST		SEPTEMBER		OCTOBER		**NOVEMBER**	
06h	05h	04h	03h	02h	01h	00h	23h	22h	**21h**	20h

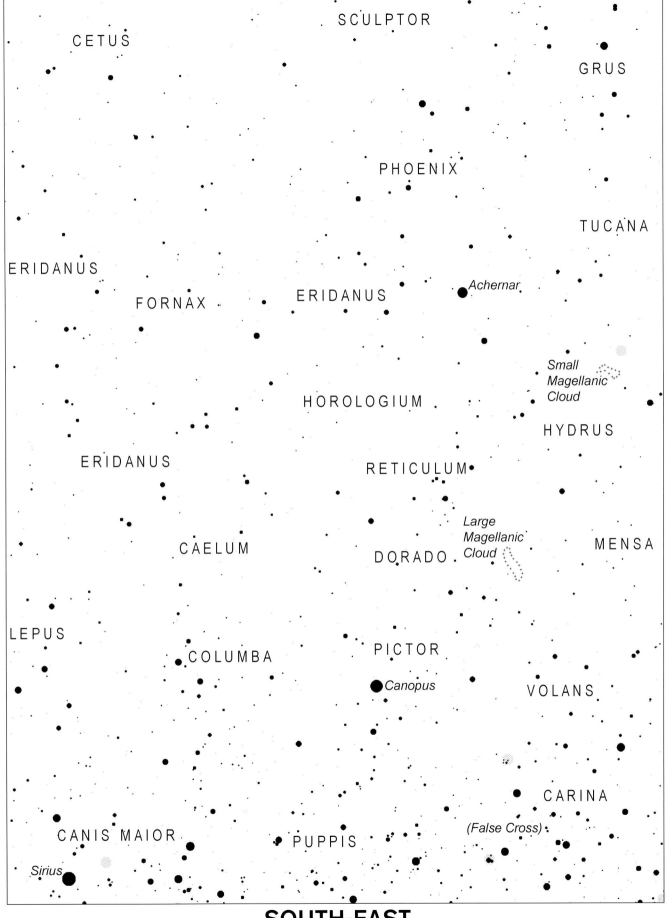

SCULPTOR

CETUS

GRUS

PHOENIX

TUCANA

ERIDANUS

FORNAX

ERIDANUS

Achernar

Small Magellanic Cloud

HOROLOGIUM

HYDRUS

ERIDANUS

RETICULUM

Large Magellanic Cloud

MENSA

CAELUM

DORADO

PICTOR

VOLANS

Canopus

LEPUS

COLUMBA

CARINA

(False Cross)

CANIS MAIOR

PUPPIS

Sirius

SOUTH-EAST

JULY	AUGUST	SEPTEMBER	OCTOBER	**NOVEMBER**	
06h 05h	04h 03h	02h 01h	00h 23h	22h **21h**	20h

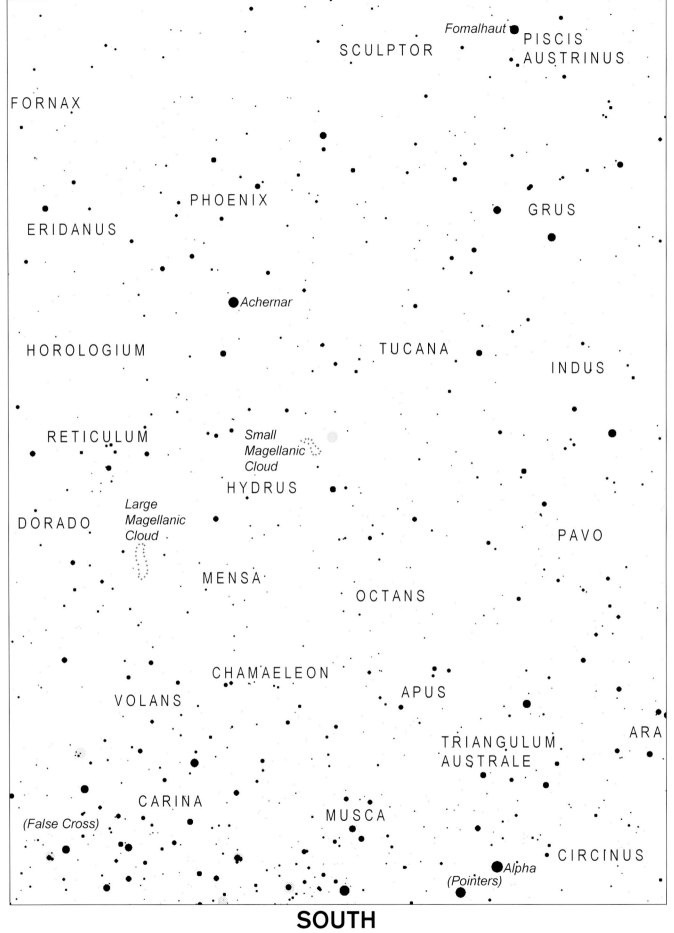

FORNAX

SCULPTOR

Fomalhaut PISCIS
AUSTRINUS

PHOENIX

ERIDANUS

GRUS

●*Achernar*

HOROLOGIUM

TUCANA

INDUS

RETICULUM

*Small
Magellanic
Cloud*

HYDRUS

DORADO

*Large
Magellanic
Cloud*

PAVO

MENSA

OCTANS

CHAMAELEON

APUS

VOLANS

TRIANGULUM
AUSTRALE

ARA

(False Cross)

CARINA

MUSCA

CIRCINUS

*Alpha
(Pointers)*

SOUTH

	JULY		AUGUST		SEPTEMBER		OCTOBER		**NOVEMBER**	
06h	05h	04h	03h	02h	01h	00h	23h	22h	**21h**	20h

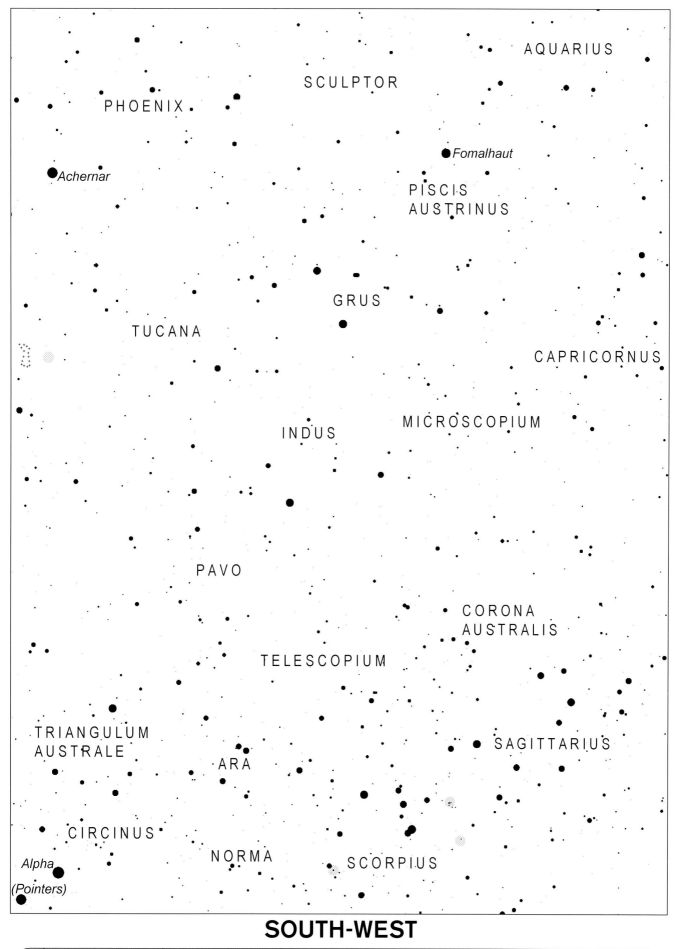

AQUARIUS

SCULPTOR

PHOENIX

Fomalhaut

●*Achernar*

PISCIS
AUSTRINUS

GRUS

TUCANA

CAPRICORNUS

MICROSCOPIUM

INDUS

PAVO

CORONA
AUSTRALIS

TELESCOPIUM

TRIANGULUM
AUSTRALE

SAGITTARIUS

ARA

CIRCINUS

NORMA

SCORPIUS

Alpha
(Pointers)

SOUTH-WEST

	JULY		AUGUST		SEPTEMBER		OCTOBER		**NOVEMBER**	
06h	05h	04h	03h	02h	01h	00h	23h	22h	**21h**	20h

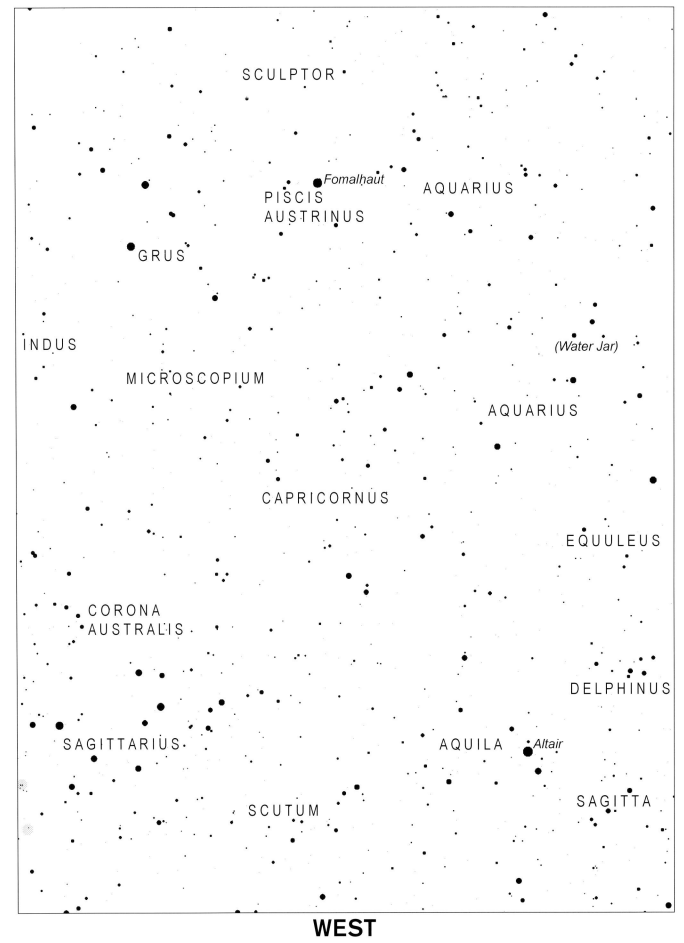

SCULPTOR

Fomalhaut

PISCIS
AUSTRINUS

AQUARIUS

GRUS

INDUS

(Water Jar)

MICROSCOPIUM

AQUARIUS

CAPRICORNUS

EQUULEUS

CORONA
AUSTRALIS

DELPHINUS

SAGITTARIUS

AQUILA   Altair

SAGITTA

SCUTUM

WEST

	JULY		AUGUST		SEPTEMBER		OCTOBER		**NOVEMBER**	
06h	05h	04h	03h	02h	01h	00h	23h	22h	**21h**	20h

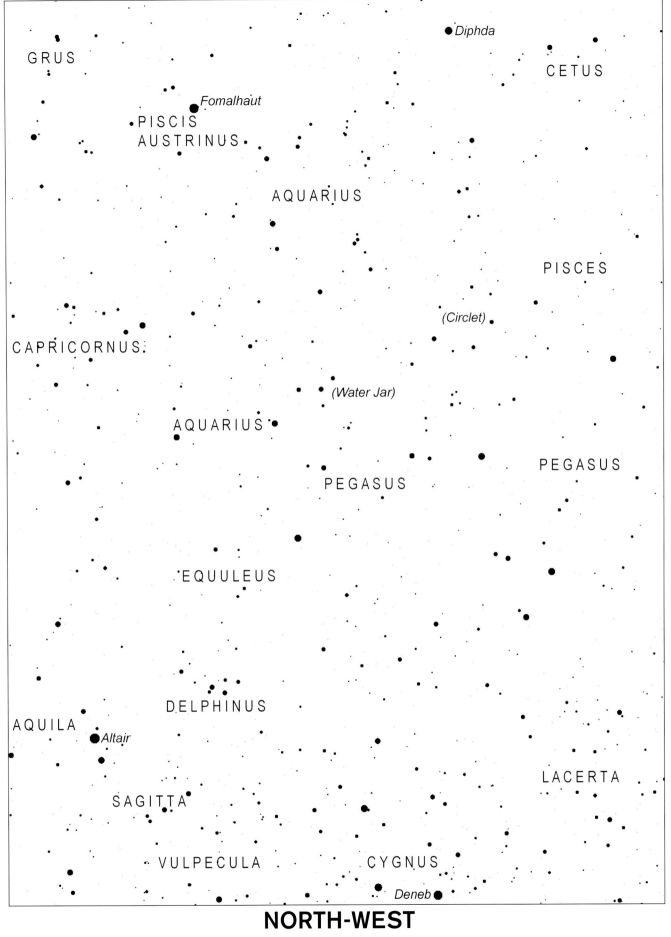

GRUS

● *Diphda*

CETUS

● *Fomalhaut*

PISCIS
AUSTRINUS

AQUARIUS

PISCES

(Circlet)

CAPRICORNUS

(Water Jar)

AQUARIUS

PEGASUS

PEGASUS

EQUULEUS

DELPHINUS

AQUILA

● *Altair*

LACERTA

SAGITTA

VULPECULA

CYGNUS

● *Deneb*

NORTH-WEST

| JULY | | AUGUST | | SEPTEMBER | | OCTOBER | | **NOVEMBER** | |
| 06h | 05h | 04h | 03h | 02h | 01h | 00h | 23h | 22h | **21h** | 20h |

SET 12
DECEMBER AT 21H

USE ALSO IN NOVEMBER AT 23H, OCTOBER AT 01H, SEPTEMBER AT 03H, AUGUST AT 05H

AT OTHER TIMES IN DECEMBER, USE: SET 1 AT 23H, SET 2 AT 01H, AND SET 3 AT 03H

HIGHLIGHT OF THE SKY TONIGHT

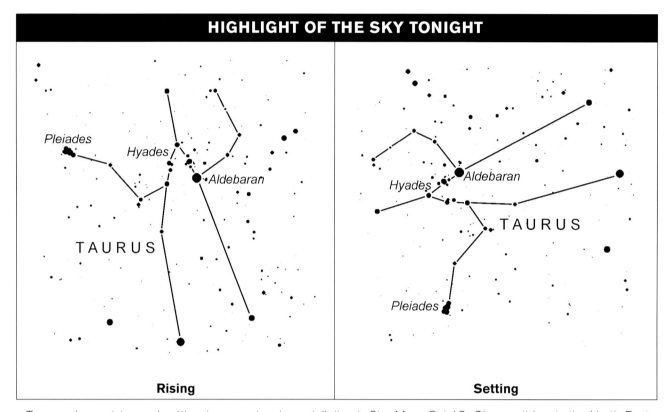

Rising

Setting

Taurus, shown rising and setting, is a prominent constellation in Star Maps Set 12. *Observe it low in the North-East.*

A guided tour of the sky

The upper part of the sky in the **North** is filled by Cetus, a large but dim constellation. Below it is the constellation of Aries. Andromeda and the constellation of Perseus are visible far below. Try to spot the Andromeda Galaxy, which is by far the most remote object you can see with the naked eye.

The bright star, Capella, in the constellation of Auriga, shines low in the **North-East**. Higher in the sky, Taurus is visible, and its red-coloured star, Aldebaran, stands out. Both the Hyades (the Rain Stars) and the Pleiades (the Seven Sisters) are beautiful when seen through binoculars. To their right is sparkling Orion, with its hot, blue Rigel and cool, red Betelgeuse shining brightly. Not far from Orion's Belt (three stars in a row) you can see the beautiful Nebula, where new stars are being created from gas and dust. Below Orion, stars of the Gemini constellation may be seen.

Sirius is the brightest star in the sky. It is striking, and shines due **East**. It is often called the Dog Star, because it belongs to the Canis Maior (the Big Dog) constellation. Just above Canis Maior are constellations Lepus and Columba. Near the horizon, Procyon shines in the Canis Minor (the Little Dog) constellation.

Canopus is almost as bright as Sirius. It shines due **South-East**, above a portion of the Milky Way that is crowded with stars. Diagonally below, the False Cross is visible. One half of the False Cross belongs to Vela, and the other forms part of Carina. This division shows that some constellation borders were 'drawn' quite arbitrarily. Canopus, for example, is taken to be a far part of Carina.

Bright Achernar shines very high in the **South**, and marks one end of the long 'river' Eridanus. The other end is close to Rigel in Orion. Both Magellanic Clouds are a little lower than the star Achernar. They are smaller galaxies than the Andromeda Galaxy, but a dozen times nearer. Therefore, they show up more clearly.

The constellation of Phoenix is on the right of Achernar, high in the **South-West**. Just below Phoenix is the constellation of Grus, which is easy to identify.

To the right of Grus, and towards the **West**, Fomalhaut shines brightly in Piscis Austrinus. Below it, you can spot Capricornus, the constellation that looks like a distorted triangle. Aquarius extends from near the horizon up to and beyond Fomalhaut. Still higher is Diphda, the brightest star in the huge but dim constellation of Cetus.

Pegasus (the Flying Horse) can be seen in the **North-West**. The four stars of the Spring Square of Pegasus are easy to identify. From here you can find your way to 'A'-shaped Pisces.

One with the stars

At the start of the Universe or the 'Absolute Zero of Time', all matter consisted of just two elements, hydrogen and helium. All other elements were later produced in stars, either during their lives (in the case of the lightest elements) or in their final moments during 'supernova' explosions (in the case of the heaviest elements).

Solid planets like the Earth are made of matter that was created and processed inside one or more stars. And what about ourselves? Yes, human beings and all other living creatures on Earth are literally shaped from stardust.

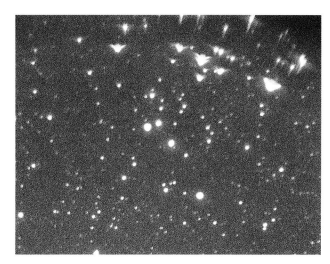

The Hyades cluster

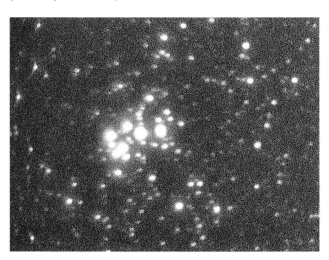

The Pleiades cluster

NEW MOON IN DECEMBER

The week around new Moon is ideal for stargazing. A December new Moon will occur:

Year	Day	Year	Day
2004	12th	2014	22nd
2005	1st & 31st	2015	11th
2006	20th	2016	29th
2007	9th	2017	18th
2008	27th	2018	7th
2009	16th	2019	26th
2010	5th	2020	14th
2011	24th	2021	4th
2012	13th	2022	23rd
2013	3rd		

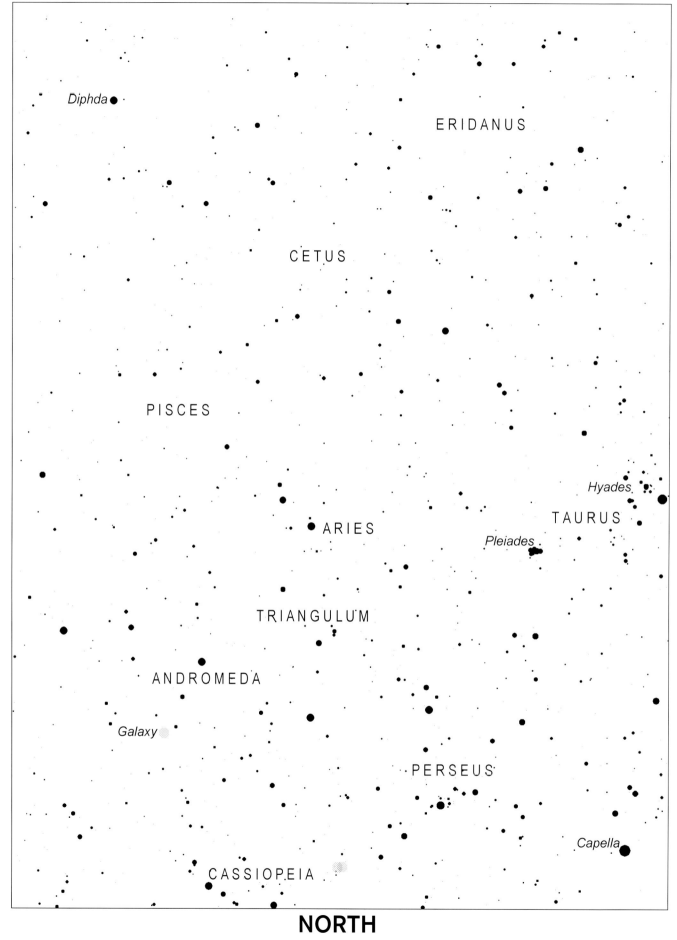

Diphda

ERIDANUS

CETUS

PISCES

Hyades

TAURUS

ARIES

Pleiades

TRIANGULUM

ANDROMEDA

Galaxy

PERSEUS

Capella

CASSIOPEIA

NORTH

	AUGUST		SEPTEMBER		OCTOBER		NOVEMBER		**DECEMBER**	
06h	05h	04h	03h	02h	01h	00h	23h	22h	**21h**	20h

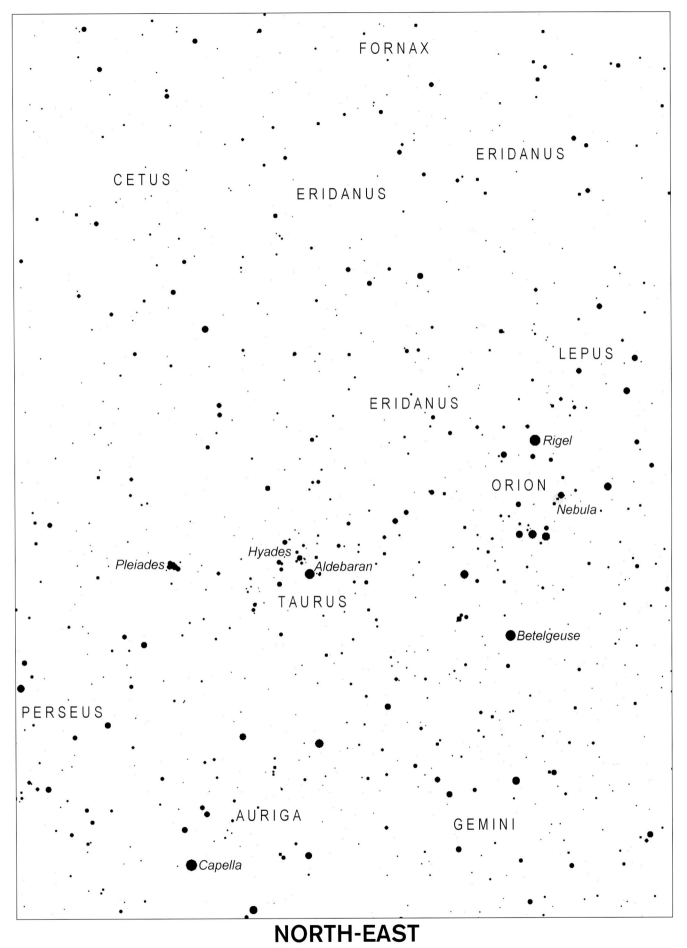

FORNAX

ERIDANUS

CETUS

ERIDANUS

LEPUS

ERIDANUS

● *Rigel*

ORION

Nebula

Hyades

Pleiades

Aldebaran

TAURUS

● *Betelgeuse*

PERSEUS

AURIGA

GEMINI

● *Capella*

NORTH-EAST

	AUGUST		SEPTEMBER		OCTOBER		NOVEMBER		DECEMBER	
06h	05h	04h	03h	02h	01h	00h	23h	22h	**21h**	20h

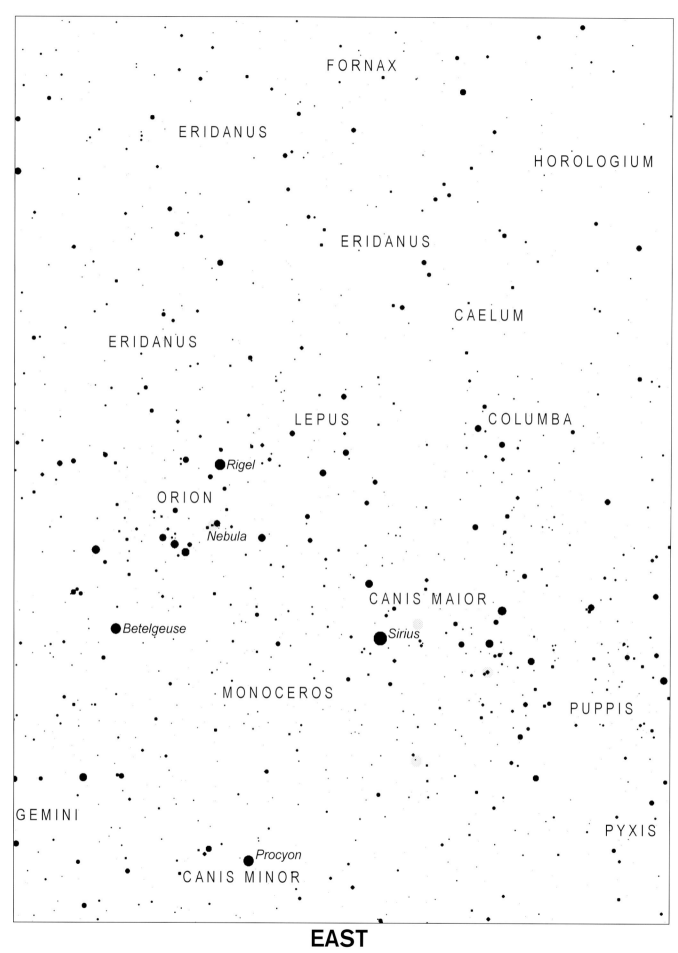

FORNAX

ERIDANUS

HOROLOGIUM

ERIDANUS

CAELUM

ERIDANUS

LEPUS

COLUMBA

●Rigel

ORION

●Betelgeuse

Nebula

CANIS MAIOR

●Sirius

MONOCEROS

PUPPIS

GEMINI

PYXIS

●Procyon

CANIS MINOR

EAST

AUGUST	SEPTEMBER	OCTOBER	NOVEMBER	**DECEMBER**	
06h 05h 04h	03h 02h	01h 00h	23h 22h	**21h**	20h

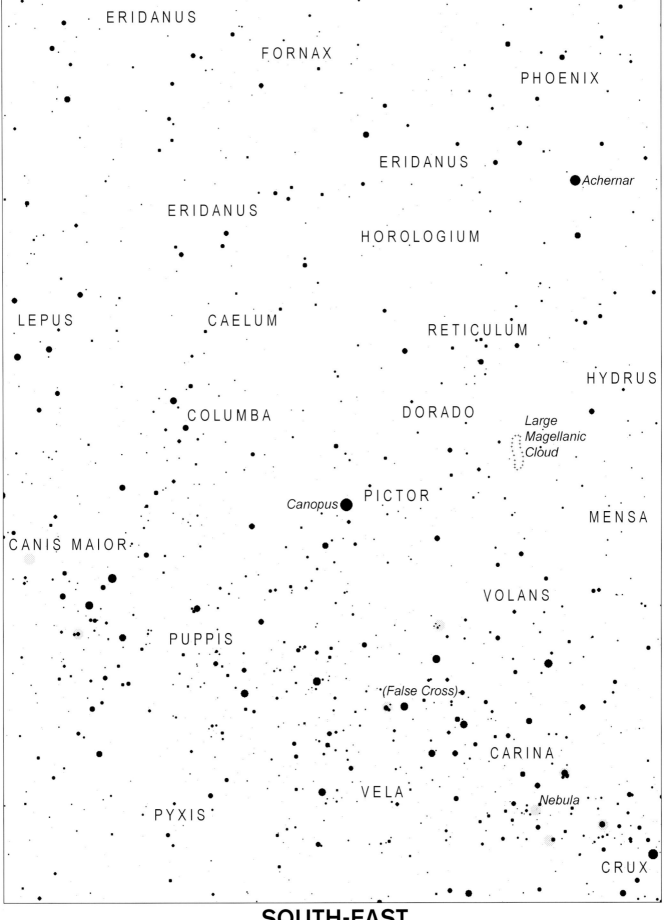

ERIDANUS

FORNAX

PHOENIX

ERIDANUS

● *Achernar*

ERIDANUS

HOROLOGIUM

LEPUS

CAELUM

RETICULUM

HYDRUS

COLUMBA

DORADO

*Large
Magellanic
Cloud*

PICTOR

Canopus ●

MENSA

CANIS MAIOR

VOLANS

PUPPIS

(False Cross)

CARINA

VELA

Nebula

PYXIS

CRUX

SOUTH-EAST

	AUGUST		SEPTEMBER		OCTOBER		NOVEMBER		**DECEMBER**	
06h	05h	04h	03h	02h	01h	00h	23h	22h	**21h**	20h

FORNAX

ERIDANUS

SCULPTOR

FRIDANUS

CAELUM

ERIDANUS

PHOENIX

HOROLOGIUM

Achernar

RETICULUM

DORADO

Canopus

PICTOR

HYDRUS

*Small
Magellanic
Cloud*

TUCANA

*Large
Magellanic
Cloud*

VOLANS

MENSA

OCTANS

CHAMAELEON

PAVO

APUS

CARINA

Nebula

MUSCA

TRIANGULUM
AUSTRALE

CRUX

ARA

SOUTH

AUGUST		SEPTEMBER	OCTOBER	NOVEMBER	DECEMBER	
06h	05h	04h	03h	02h	01h	00h	23h	22h	**21h**	20h

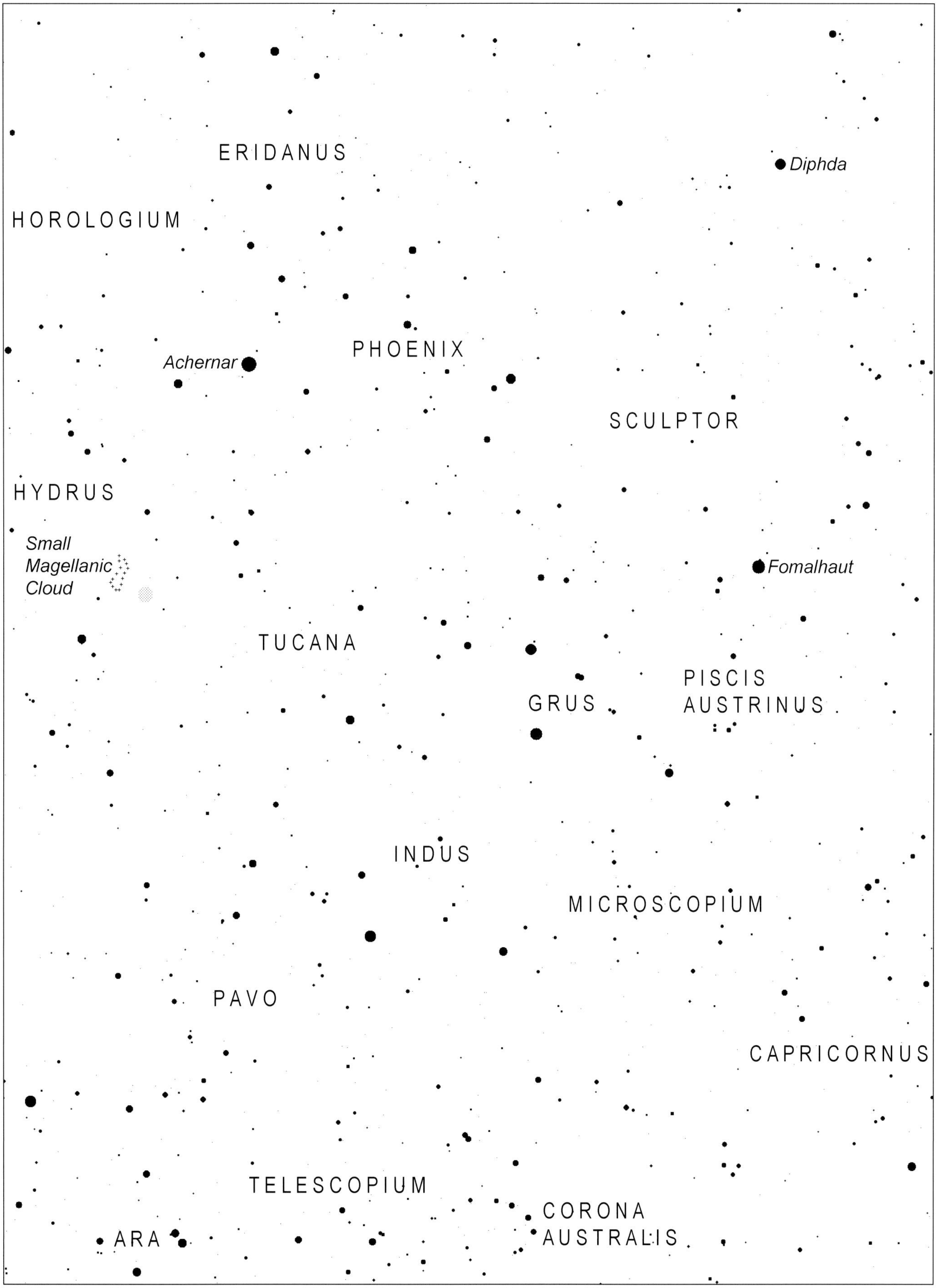

ERIDANUS

● *Diphda*

HOROLOGIUM

PHOENIX

Achernar ●

SCULPTOR

HYDRUS

*Small
Magellanic
Cloud*

● *Fomalhaut*

TUCANA

PISCIS
AUSTRINUS

GRUS

INDUS

MICROSCOPIUM

PAVO

CAPRICORNUS

TELESCOPIUM

CORONA
AUSTRALIS

ARA

SOUTH-WEST

	AUGUST		SEPTEMBER		OCTOBER		NOVEMBER		DECEMBER	
06h	05h	04h	03h	02h	01h	00h	23h	22h	**21h**	20h

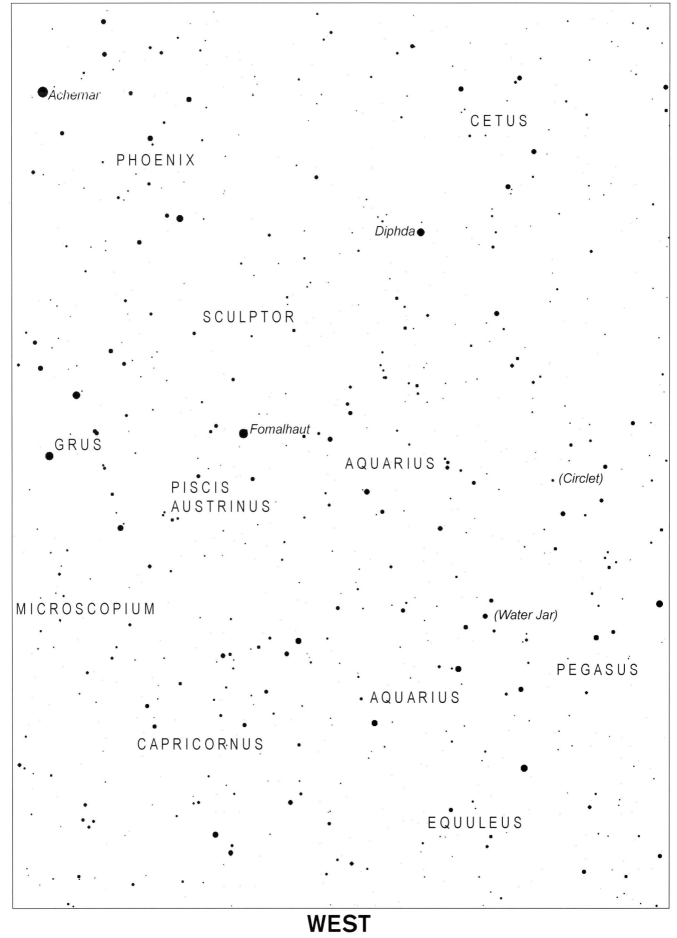

WEST

	AUGUST		SEPTEMBER		OCTOBER		NOVEMBER		**DECEMBER**	
06h	05h	04h	03h	02h	01h	00h	23h	22h	**21h**	20h

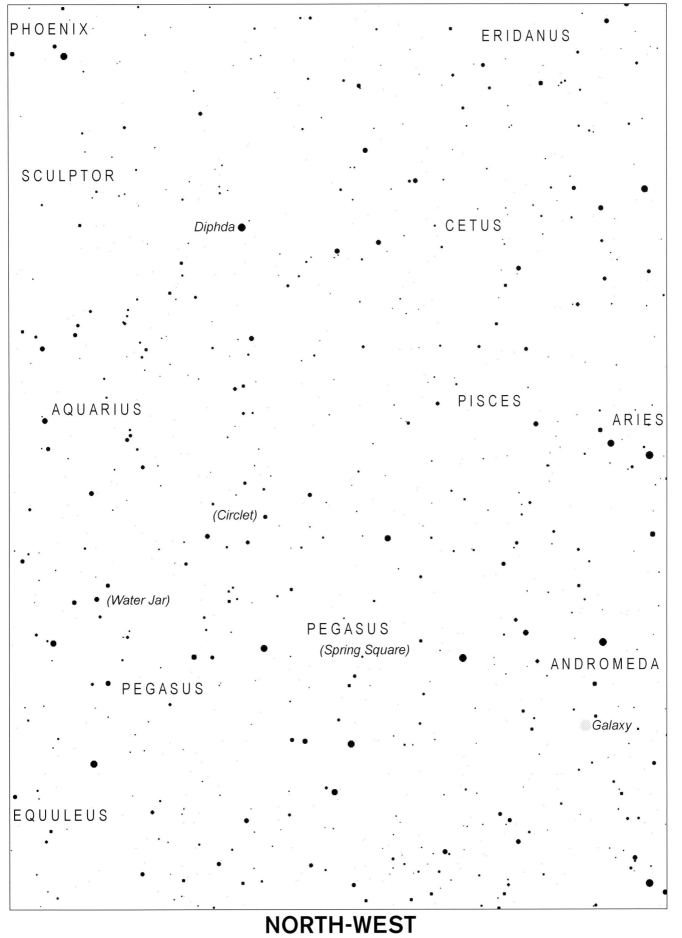

PHOENIX

ERIDANUS

SCULPTOR

CETUS

Diphda ●

PISCES

ARIES

AQUARIUS

(Circlet) ·

(Water Jar)

PEGASUS
(Spring Square)

ANDROMEDA

PEGASUS

Galaxy ·

EQUULEUS

NORTH-WEST

	AUGUST		SEPTEMBER		OCTOBER		NOVEMBER		DECEMBER	
06h	05h	04h	03h	02h	01h	00h	23h	22h	**21h**	20h

PLANETARIA AND OBSERVATORIES

Cape Town Planetarium, SA Museum (Iziko Museums), 25 Queen Victoria Street, Tel: 021 481 3900, www.museums.org.za/planetarium

Johannesburg Planetarium, Wits University, Yale Road, Milner Park, Tel: 011 717 1392, www.wits.ac.za/planetarium

South African Astronomical Observatory (SAAO), HQ: Observatory Road, Cape Town, Tel: 021 447 0025, Observing Station: nr. Sutherland, Tel: 023 571 1205, www.saao.ac.za

Boyden Observatory, Mazelspoort nr. Bloemfontein, Tel: 051 401 2924, www.uovs.ac.za/boyden

UNISA Observatory, Campus, Pretoria, Tel: 012 429 6345 or 012 429 6612, www.astro.unisa.ac.za/~uniobs

Hartebeesthoek Radio Astronomy Observatory, Tel: 012 326 0742, www.hartrao.ac.za

Port Elizabeth People's Observatory, cnr. Westview Drive/MacFarlane Road, Port Elizabeth.

Cederberg Observatory, nr. Citrusdal, Western Cape, Tel: 021 913 4200.

Prince Albert Town Observatory, 3 Market Street, Prince Albert. Tel: 023 541 1871, www.patourism.co.za

Aloe Ridge Hotel Observatory, nr. Johannesburg, Tel: 011 957 2070, www.aloeridge.com

ORGANIZATIONS

Astronomical Society of Southern Africa (ASSA)
P O Box 9, Observatory 7935. www.saao.ac.za/assa
Local centres of ASSA:
Bloemfontein Tel: 051 405 8730 or 051 436 7555, www.geocities.com/assabfn; www.spacetides.cjb.net
Cape Town Tel: 021 685 6214 or 021 447 0025.
Durban Tel: 031 564 7136 or 031 201 5829.
Garden Route Tel: 044 343 1736.
Harare www.geocities.com/zimastro
Johannesburg Tel: 011 716 3199 or 011 716 3038 www.aqua.co.za/assa_jhb
Natal Midlands Tel: 033 343 3646, www.botany.unp.ac.za/nmc/nmc.htm

Pretoria Tel: 012 333 9991, www.pretoria-astronomy.co.za
Friends of Boyden, Bloemfontein, Tel: 051 401 2924.
PE People's Observatory Society, P O Box 7988, Newton Park, Port Elizabeth 6055.
Rhodes Astronomical and Ham Radio Society, Physics Dept, Rhodes University, Grahamstown.
Astronomical Society of Bulawayo, P O Box 2365, Bulawayo, Zimbabwe.
Astronomical Work Group Namibia, P O Box 5198, Windhoek.

FURTHER READING

ASSA (ed.), *Astronomical Handbook for Southern Africa* (yearbook) (2003) ASSA, Cape Town; *Sky Guide,* (yearbook) ASSA, Cape Town (2004).

Fairall, A. *Starwatching*, Struik Publishers, Cape Town (2002).

FitzGerald, M. (ed.), *Stars of the Southern Skies*, WUP, Johannesburg (2000).

Heifetz, M. & Tirion W. *Southern Sky*, Cambridge University Press (2000).

Levy, D. *Skywatching*, Harper Collins Publishers, London (2000).

Mack, P. *Pocket Guide to the Night Skies*, Struik Publishers, Cape Town (1987).

Moore, P. *Exploring the Night Sky with Binoculars*, Cambridge University Press (2000).

Ridpath, I. & Tirion, W. *Stars and Planets*, Harper Collins Publishers, London (2000).

Tirion, W. *Cambridge Star Atlas 2000*, Cambridge University Press, (2000).

Turk, C. *Skywatching in Southern Africa*, Struik Publishers, Cape Town (2001).

INDEX TO THE MAPS

Star map set numbers are indicated in bold followed by directions

CONSTELLATIONS

Andromeda
1: NW; **10:** N, NE; **11:** N; **12:** N, NW.

Antlia
1: E, SE; **2:** E, SE; **3:** NE, E, SE, S; **4:** E, SE, S, SW; **5:** S, SW, W, NW; **6:** SW, W; **7:** SW.

Apus
1: S; **2:** S; **3:** SE, S; **4:** SE, S; **5:** SE, S; **6:** SE, S; **7:** S; **8:** S, SW; **9:** S,SW; **10:** S, SW; **11:** S; **12:** S.

Aquarius
1: W; **7:** E; **8:** NE, E; **9:** N, NE, E, NW; **10:** N, NE, E, SE, W, NW; **11:** N, SW, W, NW; **12:** W, NW.

Aquila
6: NE, E; **7:** NE, E; **8:** N, NE, E; **9:** N, NE, W, NW; **10:** W, NW; **11:** W, NW.

Ara
3:SE, S; **4:** SE; **5:** SE; **6:** SE, S; **7:** E, SE, S, SW; **8:** SE, S, SW, W; **9:** S, SW, W; **10:** S, SW; **11:** S, SW; **12:** S, SW.

Aries
1: N, NW; **2:** W, NW; **10:** NE; **11:** N, NE; **12:** N, NW.

Auriga
1: N, NE; **2:** N, NW; **3:** N, NW; **12:** NE.

Bootes
4: NE; **5:** N, NE; **6:** N, NE; **7:** N, NW; **8:** NW.

Caelum
1:SE, S, SW; **2:** S, SW, W, NW; **3:** SW, W; **4:** SW; **10:** SE; **11:** E, SE; **12:** E, SE, S.

Camelopardalis
Not visible from southern Africa.

Cancer
1: NE, E; **2:** NE; **3:** N, NE; **4:** N, NW; **5:** NW.

Canes Venatici
4: N, NE; **5:** N; **6:** N, NW; **7:** NW.

Canis Maior
1: NE, E, SE; **2:** N, NE, E, SE; **3:** N, SW, W, NW; **4:** SW, W; **5:** SW, W, **11:** E, SE; **12:** E, SE.

Canis Minor
1: NE, E; **2:** N, NE; **3:** N, NW; **4:** W, NW; **5:** W, NW; **12:** E.

Capricornus
6: E, SE; **7:** E; **8:** NE, E, SE; **9:** N, NE, E, SE, NW; **10:** N, SW, W, NW; **11:** SW, W, NW; **12:** SW, W.

Carina
1: SE, S; **2;** SE, S; **3:** SE, S, SW; **4:** SE, S, SW; **5:** S, SW; **6:** S, SW; **7:** S, SW; **8:** S, SW; **9:** S, SW; **10:** S; **11:** SE, S; **12:** SE, S.

Cassiopeia
11: N; **12:** N.

Centaurus
1: SE, S; **2:** SE; **3:** SE; **4:** E, SE, S; **5:** NE, E, SE, S, SW; **6:** SE, S, SW, W; **7:** S, SW, W; **8:** SW, W; **9:** SW.

Cepheus
Not visible from southern Africa.

Cetus
1: N, SW, W, NW; **2:** W, NW; **3:** W; **9:** E; **10:** NE, E; **11:** N, NE, E, SE, NW; **12:** N, NE, W, NW.

Chamaeleon
1: S; **2:** S; **3:** S; **4:** S; **5:** S; **6:** S, SW; **7:** S, SW; **8:** S; **9:** S; **10:** S; **11:** S; **12:** S.

Circinus
4: SE, S; **5:** SE, S; **6:** SE, S; **7:** S, SW; **8:** S, SW; **9:** SW; **10:** SW, **11:** S, SW.

Columba
1: NE, E, SE, S; **2:** SE, S, SW, W; **3:** S, SW, W, NW; **4:** SW, W, **5:** SW; **11:** E, SE; **12:** E, SE.

Coma Berenices
3: NE; **4:** N, NE; **5:** N; **6:** N, NW; **7:** NW.

Corona Australis
5: SE; **6:** E, SE; **7:** E, SE; **8:** E, SE, S; **9:** S, SW, W, NW; **10:** SW, W; **11:** SW, W; **12:** SW.

Corona Borealis
5: NE; **6:** N, NE; **7:** N; **8:** NW; **9:** NW.

Corvus
2: E, SE; **3:** E; **4:** N, NE, E, SE; **5:** N, NE, NW; **6:** N, SW, W, NW; **7:** W; **8:** SW, W.

Crater
2: E; **3:** NE, E; **4:** N, NE, E, SE; **5:** N, SW, W, NW; **6:** W, NW; **7:** W.

Crux
1: SE, S; **2:** SE, S; **3:** SE, S; **4:** SE, S; **5:** SE, S, SW;
6: S, SW; **7:** S, SW; **8:** S, SW; **9:** S, SW; **10:** S, SW;
12: SE, S.

Cygnus
7: NE; **8:** N, NE; **9:** N; **10:** N, NW; **11:** NW.

Delphinus
7: NE, E; **8:** NE; **9:** N, NE; **10:** N, NW; **11:** W, NW.

Dorado
1: SE, S, SW; **2:** S, SW; **3:** S, SW; **4:** SW; **5:** S, SW,
9: SE, S; **10:** SE, S; **11:** SE, S; **12:** SE, S.

Draco
7: N; **8:** N; **9:** N, NW.

Equuleus
7: NE, E; **8:** NE, E; **9:** N, NE; **10:** N, NW; **11:** W, NW;
12: W, NW.

Eridanus
1: N, NE, S, SW, W, NW; **2:** N, S, SW, W, NW; **3:** SW, W;
4: SW, W; **8:** SE; **9:** SE; **10:** E, SE; **11:** NE, E, SE, S;
12: All 8 maps.

Fornax
1: S, SW, W, NW; **2:** SW, W; **3:** SW, W; **9:** E, SE; **10:** E,
SE; **11:** NE, E, SE, S; **12:** NE, E, SE, S.

Gemini
1: N, NE; **2:** N, NE; **3:** N, NW; **4:** NW; **12:** NE, E.

Grus
1: SW; **2:** SW; **7:** SE; **8:** E, SE; **9:** NE, E, SE, S; **10:** E, SE,
S, SW, W; **11:** SE, S, SW, W, NW; **12:** SW, W.

Hercules
6: N, NE; **7:** N, NE; **8:** N, NW; **9:** N, NW; **10:** NW.

Horologium
1: SE, S, SW, W; **2:** S, SW, W; **3:** SW; **4:** SW; **9:** SE; **10:**
SE; **11:** SE. S; **12:** E, SE, S, SW.

Hydra
1: NE, E; **2:** NE, E, SE; **3:** N, NE, E, SE, NW; **4:** N, NE, E,
SE, S, W, NW; **5:** All 8 maps; **6:** N, SW, W, NW; **7:** SW, W,
NW; **8:** SW, W.

Hydrus
1: S, SW; **2:** S, SW; **3:** S, SW; **4:** S, SW; **5:** S;
6: S; **7:** S; **8:** SE, S; **9:** SE, S; **10:** SE, S; **11:** SE, S;
12: SE, S, SW.

Indus
1: SW; **6:** SE; **7:** SE; **8:** SE, S; **9:** E, SE, S, SW; **10:** SE, S,
SW, W; **11:** S, SW, W; **12:** SW.

Lacerta
9: N, NE; **10:** N; **11:** N, NW.

Leo
2: NE, E, **3.** N, NE, **4.** N, NE, NW, **5:** N, NW; **6:** NW;
7: W, NW.

Leo Minor
3: N, NE; **4:** N; **5:** N, NW; **6:** NW.

Lepus
1: N, NE, E, SE; **2:** N, SW, W, NW; **3:** SW, W, NW; **4:** W;
11: E, SE; **12:** NE, E, SE.

Libra
4: E; **5:** NE, E, SE; **6:** N, NE, E; **7:** N, SW, W, NW;
8: W, NW; **9:** SW, W.

Lupus
3: SE; **4:** E, SE; **5:** E, SE, S; **6:** NE, E, SE, S, SW; **7:** SE, S,
SW, W; **8:** S, SW, W; **9:** SW, W; **10:** SW.

Lynx
2: N, NE; **3:** N; **4:** N, NW; **5:** NW.

Lyra
7: N, NE; **8:** N; **9:** N, NW; **10:** NW.

Mensa
1: S; **2:** S; **3:** S, SW; **4:** S, SW; **5:** S; **6:** S; **7:** S; **8:** S; **9:** S;
10: S; **11:** SE, S; **12:** SE, S.

Microscopium
1: SW; **6:** SE; **7:** E, SE; **8:** E, SE; **9:** E, SE, S; **10:** S, SW, W,
NW; **11:** SW, W; **12:** SW, W.

Monoceros
1: NE, E; **2:** N, NE, E, NW; **3:** N, NE, W, NW; **4:** W, NW;
5: W; **12:** E.

Musca
1: SE, S; **2:** SE, S; **3:** SE, S; **4:** SE, S; **5:** SE, S, SW; **6:** S,
SW; **7:** S, SW; **8:** S, SW; **9:** S, SW; **10:** S; **11:** S; **12:** S.

Norma
3: SE; **4:** SE; **5:** SE; **6:** E, SE, S; **7:** SE, S, SW; **8:** S, SW,
W; **9:** SW, W; **10:** SW; **11:** SW.

Octans
1: S; **2:** S; **3:** S; **4:** S; **5:** S; **6:** S; **7:** S;| **8:** S; **9:** S; **10:** S;
11: S; **12:** S.

Ophiuchus
5: E; **6:** NE, E; **7:** N, NE, E, NW; **8:** N, SW, W, NW;
9: W; NW; **10:** W, NW.

Orion
1: N, NE, E, NW; **2:** N, NE, W, NW; **3:** W, NW; **4:** W;
11: E; **12:** NE, E.

Pavo
1: S, SW; **2:** S; **3:** S; **4:** SE, S; **5:** SE, S; **6:** SE, S; **7:** SE, S;
8: SE, S, SW; **9:** SE, S, SW; **10:** S, SW; **11:** S, SW;
12: S, SW.

STARS

Antares
4: E, SE; **5:** E, SE; **6:** NE, E, SE, S; **7:** N, NE, E, **8:** N, S, SW,
W, NW; **9:** SW, W; **10:** SW, W.

Arcturus
4: NE, E; **5:** N, NE; **6:** N, NE, NW; **7:** N, NW; **8:** W, NW.

Betelgeuse
1: N, NE, E; **2:** N, NE, NW; **3:** W, NW; **4:** W, NW; **11:** E;
12: NE, E.

Canopus
1: E, SE, S; **2:** E, SE, S, SW, W; **3:** SE, S, SW, W; **4:** S,
SW, W; **5:** SW; **6:** S, SW; **10:** SE, S; **11:** SE;
12: SE, S.

Capella
1: N, NE; **2:** N, NW; **3:** N, NW; **12:** N, NE.

Castor
1: NE; **2:** N, NE; **3:** N, NW; **4:** NW.

Deneb
8: N, NE; **9:** N; **10:** N, NW; **11:** NW.

Denebola
3: NE, E; **4:** N, NE; **5:** N, NW; **6:** NW; **7:** W, NW.

Diphda
1: SW, W, NW; **2:** SW, W; **8:** E, SE; **9:** E, **10:** NE, E, SE;
11: N, NE, E, NW; **12:** N, SW, W, NW.

Fomalhaut
1: SW, W; **7:** E, SE; **8:** E, SE; **9:** NE, E, SE;
10: NE, E, SE, S; **11:** S, SW, W, NW; **12:** SW, W.

Pollux
1: NE; **2:** N, NE; **3:** N, NW; **4:** N, NW; **5:** NW.

Procyon
1: NE, E; **2:** N, NE, E; **3:** N, NE, NW; **4:** W, NW;
5: W, NW; **12:** E.

Regulus
2: NE, E; **3:** N, NE; **4:** N, NE, NW; **5:** N, NW;
6: W, NW.

Rigel
1: N, NE, E, NW; **2:** N, NE, W, NW; **3:** W, NW; **4:** W;
11: E; **12:** NE, E.

Sirius
1: NE, E, SE; **2:** N, NE, E, N,W; **3:** N, SW, W, NW;
4: W, NW; **5:** SW, W; **11:** E, SE; **12:** E.

Spica
3: E; **4:** NE, E; **5:** N, NE, E, SE, NW; **6:** N, NE, W, NW;
7: W, NW; **8:** W.

Vega
7: N, NE; **8:** N; **9:** N, NW; **10:** NW.

NEBULAE, CLUSTERS & GALAXIES

Andromeda Galaxy
1: NW; **10:** N, NE; **11:** N; **12:** N, NW.

Carina Nebula
1: SE, S; **2:** SE, S; **3:** SE, S; **4:** SE, S, SW; **5:** S, SW;
6: S, SW; **7:** S, SW; **8:** S, SW; **12:** SE, S.

Hyades
1: N, NE, NW; **2:** NW; **3:** W, NW; **11:** NE, E;
12: N, NE.

Large Magellanic Cloud
1: SE, S; **2:** S, SW; **3:** S, SW;
4: S, SW; **5:** S, SW; **6:** S; **7:** S; **8:** S; **9:** S; **10:** SE, S;
11: SE, S; **12:** SE, S.

Orion Nebula
1: N, NE, E; **2:** N, NE, W, NW; **3:** W, NW;
4: W; **11:** E; **12:** NE, E.

Pleiades
1: N, NW; **2:** NW; **3:** W, NW; **11:** NE; **12:** N, NE.

Small Magellanic Cloud
1: S, SW; **2:** S, SW; **3:** S, SW; **4:** S; **5:** S; **6:** S; **7:** S; **8:** SE,
S; **9:** SE, S; **10:** SE, S; **11:** SE, S; **12:** S, SW.

COMMON NAMES

Circlet
1: W; **8:** E; **9:** NE, E; **10:** N, NE; **11:** N, NW;
12: W, NW.

False Cross
1: SE; **2:** SE, S; **3:** SE, S, SW; **4:** S, SW;
5: S, SW; **6:** SW; **7:** SW; **11:** SE, S; **12:** SE.

Northern Cross
8: N, NE; **9:** N; **10:** N, NW.

Pointers
1: S; **2:** SE, S; **3:** SE, S; **4:** SE, S; **5:** SE, S;
6: SE, S, SW; **7:** S, SW; **8:** S, SW; **9:** S, SW; **10:** S, SW;
11: S, SW.

Sickle
2: NE; **3:** N, NE; **4:** N, NW; **5:** NW; **6:** NW.

Southern Cross
1: SE, S; **2:** SE, S; **3:** SE, S; **4:** SE, S;
5: SE, S, SW; **6:** S, SW; **7:** S, SW; **8:** SW; **9:** S, SW.

Spring Square
9: NE; **10:** N, NE; **11:** N; **12:** NW.

Water Jar
1: W; **8:** NE, E; **9:** NE, E; **10:** N, NE, E, NW;
11: N, W, NW; **12:** W, NW.